SEXOLOGY

OR

STARTLING SINS OF THE STERNER SEX

PRICE $2.00

BY

GEO. F. HALL,

AUTHOR OF

"The Lord's Exchequer," "Some American Evils and
Their Remedies," etc.

THE L. W. WALTER COMPANY
CHICAGO, ILL.

DEDICATORY.

To every man, both great and small,
Whether young or old,
Whether white or black,
Whether rich or poor,
Whether strong or weak,
Whether saint or sinner,
This volume is respectfully inscribed by on
who desires to enlist the active sympathies
of all in behalf of a nobler manhood.

AUTHORITIES CITED.

Addison
Arnold
Arvine
Augustine
Badeau
Bailley
Barnum
Barrow
Beaconsfield
Beaumetz
Bible
Bovee
Brandt
Brodie
Bryant
Buckley
Burrows
Cameron
Caton
Chase
Cicero
Clokey
Coles
Columbus
Comstock
Cowan
Dix
Dixon
Drysdale
Dwight
Ellis
Ely
Emerson
Everest
Fairchild

Franklin
Galen
Garfield
Geike
Gladstone
Green
Griswold
Guernsey
Hall
Haynes
Hippocrates
Howe
Hughes
Kellogg
Lallemand
Langford
La Rochefoucauld
Laws of Life
Leonard
Leopold
Lewis
Livesey
London Times
Longfellow
Lowber
Lowell
McArthur
McCandlass
Meredith
Milton
Moore
Napoleon
Newton
Nott
Parker

Parkes
Paul
Payne
Phillips
Pope
Pope (Dr.)
Potter
Prince
Psychological
    Journal
Republic
Richardson
Rush
Scott
Seerly
Sherman
Silliman
Smith
Solomon
Spaulding
Steele
Stewart
Swift
Talmage
Tappan
Taylor
Tennyson
Todd
Updike
Waite
Watts
Wayland
Webster
Wilcox
Windom

TABLE OF CONTENTS.

INTRODUCTORY.

CHAPTER IV.—TOBACCO, OR HEATHENDOM'S
MOST POPULAR GIFT TO CHRISTENDOM.

CHAPTER V.—BAD BOOKS AND PICTURES.

INTRODUCTORY.

Without meaning any disrespect whatever to the gentler sex, I am profoundly thankful that I was not born to wear petticoats. I would rather be a man than anything else in the universe, angels not excepted. I never sing that old song,

> "I want to be an angel,
> And with the angels stand, etc.,"

for I don't want to be an angel. I want to be simply a man,—a plain man, a true man, a pure man, a redeemed MAN!

We learn in the first chapter of the Book of Genesis that God created man in his own image. What a magnificent honor! How careful we should be to preserve this image in all its strength and beauty.

But man is a careless being. He is very much inclined to sinful things. He more often does that which is wrong than that which is right, because it is easier,

and, for the moment, perhaps, more sat-
isfying to the flesh. The Creator is often
blamed for man's weaknesses and incon-
sistencies. This is wrong. God did not
intend that we should be mere machines,
but free moral agents. We are privileged
to choose between good and evil. Hence,
if we perversely choose the latter, and
make a miserable failure of life, we should
blame only ourselves.

After optimism has done its best to
throw a halo of glory about the present
age, the fact still remains that this is a
very wicked old world. I do not mean
to insinuate that the world is not growing
better. It is—*in spots*. It is also growing worse in spots. The important question is, *Which spot are you in?*

I have written this little volume to help
my brothers everywhere. I want to see
them make improvement in everything
that's good. Want to see them have
stronger bodies, stronger minds, and
stronger characters. Want to see them
live longer and happier. Want to see
them make the most of life, and come to
their journey's end in the full flush of an
immortal victory. One of the most press-

ing wants of the age is for MEN—men of
genuine worth, physically, mentally, and
spiritually; men of unwavering personal
purity in every particular. I hope these
pages will help in some measure to supply the demand. I believe the Gospel of
Jesus Christ was intended to make the
race better everyway. That religion
which fails to take in the whole being—
body, soul, and spirit—is not worthy to be
called after Christ. Therefore I have no
apology to offer for speaking along lines
of thought usually ignored by ministers.
I feel it to be my duty. Would that
every pulpit in the land might join hands
with the medical profession and cry out
with no uncertain sound against the
mighty evils herein stigmatized! It
would work a revolution for which coming society could never cease to be
grateful. "Moses, learned in the knowledge of the Egyptians, not only pub-
licly announced the moral law for the
guidance of man's social life," says Dr.
Pope, "but also gave excellent precau-
tions against the spread of sickness, and
rules by which the body might be maintained in health and integrity. *It is an*

undeniable fact that moral impotence usually denotes neglect of physical welfare."

The time has arrived for a full and frank discussion of those things which affect the personal purity of men. Thousands are suffering to-day from various weaknesses, the causes of which they have never learned. Manly vigor is not increasing with that rapidity which a Christian age demands. Means of dissipation are on the increase. It is high time, therefore, that every lover of the race should call a halt, and inquire into the condition of things. Excessive modesty on this subject is not a virtue. Timidity in presenting unpleasant but important truths has permitted untold damage in every age. I have endeavored, therefore, to speak the truth plainly and boldly, and devoutly hope that my labors will result in the transformation of many characters for their present and eternal welfare.

Oh, brother, be manly! Strive to attain unto a higher and better life. Beware of all excesses, of whatever nature, and guard your personal purity with sacred determination. Let every aspiration be upward, and be strong in every good resolution. Seek the light, for in light there is life, while in darkness there is decay and death. Tennyson wisely wrote:

"Self-reverence, self-knowledge, self-control,
These three alone lead life to sovereign power."

God give us men!   A time like this demands
Strong minds, great hearts, true faith and ready hands !
—*Holland.*

CHAPTER I.

THE STRONGEST MAN IN THE WORLD.

SAMSON is commonly spoken of as the strongest man that ever lived, and John L. Sullivan as the strongest man of modern times. But this is not true, except in a very limited and inferior sense. Samson and Sullivan are names now almost uniformly associated with muscle, but not with noble character.

Sullivan wore the championship belt as the world's greatest pugilist for more than ten years, and yet he is not strong enough to resist a glass of whisky, or the fulsome praise of his boon companions, which, if possible, is more debilitating in effect upon him than the liquor.

And so with Samson. He was strong enough to slay a lion, kill a thousand

Philistines with the jaw bone of an ass, carry off the heavy gates of the city of Gaza, and to do many other marvelous things, and yet he was not strong enough to resist the enticements of a lewd woman. Through the evil machinations of Delilah, the great giant was shorn of his hair, and thus lost his matchless strength of muscle.

"But," says my sceptical friend, "it is asking too much for me to believe that the strength of a man lies in long hair." I do not ask you to believe that. Samson's great strength did not lie in his hair literally, but in a principle. In the Book of Judges, thirteenth chapter, we read, "And there was a certain man of Zorah, of the family of the Danites, whose name was Manoah; and his wife was barren, and bare not. And the Angel of the Lord appeared unto the woman, and said unto her: Behold now, thou art barren, and bearest not, but thou shalt conceive, and bear a son. Now therefore beware, I pray thee, and drink not wine nor strong drink, and eat not any unclean thing. For, lo, thou shalt conceive, and bear a son; and no razor shall come on his head, for the child shall be a Nazarite unto God from the womb; and he shall begin to deliver Isreal out of the hands of the Philistines." God raised up Samson for a certain important work, and gave him the strength necessary to do that work. But he should retain his strength only on certain conditions: he should allow no razor to come upon his head; should eat no unclean thing; and should abstain from wine. He should live the life of a Nazarite, and just so long as he observed this law of his Maker with reference to himself, just so long was he able for every great task. But the moment he violated Divine principle, that moment he became a weak man.

Edgar Allan Poe, Lord Byron and Robert Burns were men of marvelous strength intellectually. But measured by the true rule of high moral principle, they were very weak. Superior endowment in a single direction — physical, mental or spiritual — is not of itself sufficient to make one strong in all that that heroic word means.

Many a good man spiritually has gone

to an untimely grave because of impaired
physical powers. Many a good man
spiritually has gone to the insane asylum
because of bodily and mental weaknesses.
Many a good man spiritually has fallen
from virtue in an evil moment because of
a weakened will, or, a too demanding
fleshly passion, or, worse than either, too
lax views on the subject of personal
chastity.

Who, then, is the strongest man in the
world? I answer, *he who most symmet-
rically and vigorously develops body, soul
and spirit, and who lives most nearly in
accordance with the eternal principles set
forth in the Book of God.* Every reader of
these lines, therefore, may become one of
the strongest men in the world. You may
never be as muscular as Sullivan, or as
intellectual as Byron, or as spiritual as
Spurgeon; but you may be able to better
combine and harmoniously develop these
several elements of strength. If so, you
may confidently expect to be one of the
happiest and strongest of men in all that
constitutes true manhood.

It is said that the ancient Greeks wrote
this maxim over the portals of their tem-

ples dedicated to Hygeia: *Mens sana in corpore sano* (a sound mind in a sound body). This was a wise suggestion. Would that I could write it upon the tablets of every man's memory to-day.

Physical and moral degeneracy is the bane of this age. The words of the great apostle to the Gentiles to the young preacher Timothy, "Keep thyself pure," were never more appropriate than now. This commandment of three words enwraps the secret of manly strength. In another chapter, penned to the same individual, Paul said, "Flee also youthful lusts, but follow righteousness, faith, charity, peace, with them that call on the Lord out of a pure heart." The man who ignores this inspired advice, whether in whole or in part, should never expect to be rated a strong man. But for him who accepts it and acts accordingly, Heaven only knows what rich things are in store, both for time and eternity.

CHAPTER II.

CAUSES OF PHYSICAL AND MORAL DEGENERACY.

It is a well-known fact that people usually do not like to look on the dark side of things. They do not like to be told of their faults. They want preachers, teachers and everybody to tickle rather than switch. I am frank to confess that this is the case with myself. And yet I know that many times in my life, fate, or some other power, has tickled me, when a switching, perhaps, would have been much more appropriate.

I shall have to do some switching in this work. Much as we love to look only on the brighter side of life, we must at times look on the darker. He who does not, has no right to claim to be the friend of his race. The true friend of humanity points out the pitfalls of life, as well as its green pastures and still waters.

Some timid souls have objected to works of this nature on the ground that " where ignorance is bliss, 'tis folly to be

wise." They argue that boys and young
men will read the book and learn of vices
concerning which they had never so much
as dreamed before. Well, so mote it be.
If I can clearly describe, and in frightful
colors paint, some of the secret as well as
open sins which are blighting the men of our
generation, and thus make plain to all the
path of duty, I feel sure that thousands
of as yet undefiled youths will rise up and
bless my labors for opening their eyes to
danger, though their over-modest parents
consider me too bold.

The fact is clearly visible on every
hand that the physical and moral manhood of the race is not what it should be.
Indeed, with a considerable part of the
world, it may be seriously questioned if it
is what it once was. The present generation is notorious for its small-bodied and
weak-principled men. It is notorious for
its dissipating and demon-like men—men
indeed "whose end is destruction, whose
God is their belly, and whose glory is in
their shame, who mind earthly things."
Men are dying much more rapidly than
women proportionately, chiefly because
their disregard of personal purity in its

various phases is greater. The vast majority of the graduates from the public schools and colleges of the land to-day, and two-thirds of the memberships of our churches, are females. In competitive examinations everywhere girls are carrying off most of the prizes. Why is it? Because the gentler sex dissipates less. That is why. Because, as a sex, women have maintained in a more perfect degree their personal purity against the weakening dissipations to which men yield themselves with such loose rein.

Which sex furnishes almost the entire number of criminals for the cells of our penitentiaries? Is it not the sex that patronizes more freely the saloons, gambling dens, brothels, tobacco stores, and other vile pits of impurity? And are not these pits rapidly increasing in number, efficiency for evil, and popularity with the masses? An ex-warden of the state penitentiary at Joliet, Ill., recently stated that while the population of his state has increased twenty-five per cent. in the past few years, its crime has increased forty per cent. And as our criminal population is made up almost entirely of males, is it not high time that earnest, thoughtful inquiry was being made as to the cause of this startling degeneracy?

It has been estimated that seventy-five per cent. of the young men of this country do not darken a church door from one month's end to another, and only five per cent. are professing Christians. This does not augur well for the future of our republic. Much of the business of our country, commercial and professional, is in the hands of young men, who, in a few short years, must control it all. To-day they occupy positions of trust in our stores, counting houses, factories, institutions of learning, pulpits, etc. To-morrow, they will be looked to for leadership in all the departments of human activity. What can the world expect of them if they come into this larger sphere with weakened bodies, and still more weakened morals— weakened by indulgence in every form of physical and mental dissipation?

The world is full of good places for the right men. It is true that tens of thousands of men, young, middle-aged and old, put in much of their time scrambling for a place. But they are incompetent. There are many places of trust and honor scrambling for good men, true men, pure men, strong men—men who are thoroughly competent in every particular. Such men never seek long for a place. There is no greater barrier to one's advancement and success than personal impurity, which is the mother of incompetency.

For six thousand years, the human race, as a race, has been slowly ascending the hill of progress. In some things, 'tis true, we are not as well off as by-gone generations; but in many other things, we are infinitely better off. This is undoubtedly, everything considered, the grandest age of the world so far, thanks be to the comparatively few men of principle, who, under God, have saved each generation from total ruin. The great question is, Shall we have more men of principle, and so hold what has been gained, and go on to even greater heights of prosperity? Or shall we give over to the god of impurity, and retrograde? Personally, I believe that there are better times ahead. There is more agitation on the subject of principle to-day than ever before, and I believe it was Wendell Phillips who said that "agitation is half a victory."

The Greeks and Romans were especially noted for their physical prowess. The former had their Olympian games, and the latter their gladiatorial conquests. For thousands of years, the physical had as much, and often more, to do with a man's promotion or downfall at the hands of his countrymen as the mental or moral. Saul was selected first king of Israel on account of his being a head and shoulders taller than any other man in the nation. Coming further down the centuries, we find that the intellectual figured more prominently in human greatness than the physical. And this continues in large measure even to the present. When speaking of Luther, Milton, Shakespeare, Pitt, Cromwell, Burke, Napoleon, Washington, Franklin, Webster, Garfield, etc., we do not admire them so much because they were more remarkable than many other men physically, for they were not, but because they were men of giant intellectual prowess. We are now passing rapidly into a moral age. To-day

we talk more about the right and wrong
of a thing than ever before, and the
spirit of arbitration is abroad in the land.
The sign is good. It promises the hasten-
ing on of the universal reign of Christ—
the spiritual age.

But now why not pay careful attention
to man in all his elements of strength,
physical, mental and moral? Why not
make personal purity a fixed principle in
the manhood of the present and coming
generations, and thus insure the best men
the world has ever seen? It can be done.
Let every reader of these lines resolve
that he will be one to help do it.

It is not the few especially that I am
after with these deductions, but the many.
Not the few tens of thousands who live in
the bright spots of the world's higher
development, but the many millions who
are physically and morally retrograding
in the huge black spots of human depravity—the great hissing, seething caldrons
of physical, mental and spiritual impurity.
I want to throw out to them the life-line
of knowledge, and ring the buoy-bell of
warning.

Well, to be more specific, what are the

prime causes of the physical and moral degeneracy of our nineteenth century manhood? I shall speak of the six which I consider most prolific, as follows: First, strong drink; Second, tobacco; Third, bad books and pictures; Fourth, gambling; Fifth, the social evil; Sixth, the secret vice. I have not purported to arrange these evils in the order of their importance at all. There is no need of any comparison. They are all bad enough, God knows. The devil certainly has a controlling interest in them all, and whether this is the best arrangement or not, I hope to make his majesty gnash and snarl somewhat over the plain truths I shall speak concerning these six productive plants.

CHAPTER III.

STRONG DRINK; OR, THE DEVIL IN LIQUID FORM.

Among the causes of physical and moral degeneracy in our nineteenth century manhood, strong drink is one of the most potent. Strong drink is the devil in liquid form. Its use is the source of untold misery, and no words can adequately describe the evil. While I write these sentences, strong drink is stealthily getting in its hellish work on tens of thousands of men and youths—weakening body, sapping intellect, besmirching soul, and blighting prospects. Strong drink is ruining men everywhere—cursing its multitudes both for time and eternity. I have no soft words for the business.

By strong drink, I mean every form of intoxicating drink, every liquid used as a beverage, such as alcohol, whisky, brandy, rum, gin, ale, beer, and all fermented wines. They all belong to the same family, and, in character and capacity for degrading their victims, are much alike.

Old Alcohol, however, is the father of the outfit, and most responsible for the pitiful condition of the poor mortals who have fallen into the clutches of the family. So it is against him particularly that I would direct these strictures, for if we could kill him, his children would succumb without a struggle, as they would have no heart for further operations.

I would array strong drink against the personal purity of men first, because it is a poison. Numerous cases of almost instant death from drinking a considerable quantity of pure alcohol have occurred. It might be better for society if those addicted to the use of strong drink would just take a large dose of pure alcohol and be done with it. It would prevent many heart-aches and tears. But Satan always has a sharp eye to business, and knows that such an event would be ruinous to his plans. So he has his agents mix the pure alcohol in many different forms, thus weakening its terrible sting, and permitting the drinker to live on awhile. Dr. Kellogg says "the effect is largely determined by the degree of dilution in which the poison is introduced into the system."

This poison is sure death to plants
and animals. Pour a solution of alcohol
on a plant and its leaves will soon wither
and change their color, and, although the
proportion of the poison to the water is
as one to one thousand, the plant dies. It
takes about one minute to kill a tadpole
by immersion in alcohol. Some time ago,
a French physician conducted some experiments to determine the influence of
rum on fowls. A New York journal, commenting on his report, says: "He administered to them brandy and absinthe,
and found one and all to take so kindly to
their unwonted stimulants that he was
forced to limit each bird to a daily allow-
ance of six cubic centimeters of spirits, or
twelve of wine. There was an extraordinary development of cocks' crests and
a rapid and general loss of flesh. The
experiments were continued until it appeared that two months' absinthe drinking sufficed to kill the strongest cock or
hen; while the brandy-drinkers lived four
months and a half, and the wine-bibbers
held on for ten months before they died
the drunkard's death." Dr. Kellogg, in
his splendid work entitled "Man the Mas-

terpiece," gives the following pregnant paragraph:

"Some Pennsylvania beer-sellers tried the effects of beer upon a goat. Whether the experiment was for the purpose of determining the quality of the beer, or the constitutional toughness of the goat, is not recorded; but the result was fatal to the goat, notwithstanding the hardihood for which he is proverbial. Just how many glasses were required to extinguish him is not mentioned; but he died, and the high quality of the beer was established beyond the possibility of cavil! But this is not the end of the story. The Humane Society heard of the proceeding, and immediately began an action against the beer-venders for cruelty to animals. The action was undoubtedly justifiable, but it is a matter of wonderment that the same law-makers who have made it an offense to kill goats with beer have never once thought of its being a crime to kill human beings by the same means, although there are millions of human beings sacrificed in this way to one goat. It is to be hoped that the question of prohi-

bition will be agitated until human beings
are at least as well protected as goats."

Dr. Beaumetz, of Paris, after experi-
menting several years, avers that the
effects of alcohol upon pigs is "uniformly
that of a poison." I refer to the animal
of lower creation, not to the human pig!
The effect, however, is the same upon the
latter. Some one has said that, "If lower
animals were addicted to the drug to one-
tenth the degree man is, in a short time
there would not remain upon the face of
the earth an animal which would be tam-
able, workable, or eatable."

Take a drop of pure alcohol and place
upon a raw surface of the body and witness the effect. It causes intense suffering. Alcohol is a most dangerous irri-
tant. No wonder its constant use drives
thousands into that terrible disease known
as delirium tremens.

Alcohol poisons the blood, paralyzes
the nerves of the stomach, and hardens
the brain. Medical students are always
happy when they can secure the brain of
an old toper for dissection. It is said to
be a very difficult undertaking to dissect
a healthy brain without maligning its

structure. A very sharp knife and a steady hand are required to perform the task successfully. But not so with a drunkard's brain. It is always found to be hard, and is easily cut.

The stomach of a person dying of delirium tremens is usually found, upon a *post mortem* examination, to be black with mortification. In a healthy state, the stomach presents a bright, rosy tint. The drunkard's stomach is infested with ugly ulcers. As the stomach is the headquarters of digestion, it will be readily seen that the results of drinking rum cannot but be injurious to the whole system.

Strong drink affects the heart. Dr. Parkes, by careful experiment, is reported to have ascertained that "the pulse of a man whose heart beats about seventy-four times a minute, or 106,560 times in twenty-four hours, when drinking only water, was, when under the influence of one ounce of alcohol per day, compelled to beat 430 times more in a day. Two ounces of alcohol per day caused an increase of 1,872 beats a day. Four ounces required 12,960 extra beats a day. Six ounces drove the pulse up to 18,432 extra beats; and eight ounces to 25,488 unnecessary beats, or nearly one-quarter more than when taking only water." What a fearful waste of vital energy!

It is amazing how many arguments, socalled, the lovers of rum advance in favor of its use. Some say it is a food, and cite instances where persons have been known to live for several weeks on alcohol and water. But this is no proof. There are numerous instances on record of individuals living longer on water alone. In 1876 the International Medical Congress, probably the highest medical body in the world, reported as follows: "*First*— Alcohol is not shown to have any definite food value by any of the usual methods of chemical analysis or physiological investigation. *Second*—Its use as a medicine is chiefly as a cardiac (relating to the heart) stimulant, and often admits of substitution. *Third*—Even as a *medicine*, it is not well fitted for *self preservation* by the laity."

Some say that alcohol is good for regulating the temperature of the body. Men drink it in the summer to keep cool, and in winter to keep warm. Marvelous remedy! By disturbing the circulation, drink causes an apparent increase of heat for a little time. But the thermometer always shows a decrease in the temperature. Dr. Parkes says that "all observers condemn the use of spirits, even of wine or beer, as a preventive against cold." And Dr. Kellogg asserts that "the names of Dr. King, Dr. Kane, Capt. Kennedy, and Dr. Hayes, may be cited as holding this opinion. In the last expedition in search of Sir John Franklin, the whole crew were teetotalers."

Some say that, whatever else may be said, alcohol is a good medicine. and will always be required in the treatment of various diseases. So are quinine, aconite, belladonna, strychnine, and other poisons good medicine in some cases. But who would think of using these powerful drugs as a beverage? If quinine cures my ague, must I keep on taking it all my life, in larger and larger doses, until my whole being is impaired for both time and eternity? It is a mooted question whether alcohol is necessary at all in the treatment of diseases. The following clipping, entitled "A Doctor's Prescription on

Whisky," contains more truth than poetry:

" Indiscreet people frequently rush to whisky in many diseases. It has absolutely no curative power. It may make people oblivious to disease while the effect is on, but disease goes on all the same. It inflames every coating and membrane it comes in contact with. It quickens circulation, but at the same time enters into and poisons the blood. It attacks the brain, brutalizes the mind, makes life wretched by its horrid demands for 'more,' and turns peaceful death into a terrible departure and hell. Whisky never cured any disease, but has engendered thousands. It has its place in nature, but not as a remedy for disease. It is ruinous to trifle with it, for it leads down into the bottomless pit of hell."

At the Washingtonian Home in Chicago, where thousands of cases of various natures have been treated during the past few years, no alcohol whatever is used. I have been a healthy, active man most of my life, and I have never, for any purpose whatever, medical or otherwise, taken into my stomach a draught of rum. If I should be bitten by a rattlesnake, I might indulge! But I can think of nothing else that would tempt me to let a drop of the accursed stuff pass my lips.

By the way, I remember hearing a friend relate a peculiar incident which occurred in Riley County, Kan., a few years ago. An old German farmer, working about his fences one day, accidentally pricked his hand upon a barb. By some strange fancy, he concluded that he had been snake-bitten. Having great faith in whisky as a panacea for all the ills that flesh is heir to, particularly snake-bites, the old gentleman hastened to take in all he could hold of the remedy. As may be imagined, the result was speedy death. Whisky is just as fatal as the fangs of a serpent, if taken in sufficient quantities.

Dr. Kellogg truthfully remarks that "it was long ago observed that drunkards were the favorite victims of cholera, the plague, sun-stroke, and other causes of speedy death. The system is prepared, by the paralyzing influence of the drug, for almost any form of disease." Strong drink often causes consumption, apoplexy, and dropsy. It has been dem-

onstrated that beer is a fruitful cause of
Bright's Disease. In short, rum is the
sworn enemy of the human system, and
the man who uses the vile preparation
does so at the risk of his life. Dr. Howe
charges one-half the cases of idiocy in
Massachusetts to intemperance. He cites
one instance that ought to be burned into
the conscience of every liquor drinker in
the land. In one family, where both parents were drunkards, there were seven
idiot children! Heaven pity the posterity
of those who habitually imbibe rum,
which Chancellor Dungan appropriately
nick-names "hell-stuff."

Strong drink deranges the liver. Strong
drink befouls the breath. Strong drink
weakens muscular power. It is a well-
known fact that pugilists, pedestrians,
and oarsmen are required, by the most
successful trainers, to abstain from liquors,
as well as to keep themselves from sexual
indulgence, for some time previous to
prize contests. Strong drink causes much
of the insanity with which this poor
world is afflicted. Indeed, the man who
drinks to excess but once will be insane
so long as the effect of the liquor lasts, for

the influence of strong drink upon the mental faculties is such as to completely derange the mind for a time. An intoxicated man should be pitied the same as one temporarily insane. Strong drink shortens life. "Dr. Willard Parkes, of New York," says Kellogg, "shows from statistics that for every ten temperate persons who die between the ages of twenty-one and thirty, fifty-one intemperate persons die. Thus it appears that the mortality of liquor-users is *five hundred per cent.* greater than that of temperate persons. These tables are based on tables used by Life insurance companies."

Strong drink is one of the most common causes of the all-too-frequent vitiation of family stock. On this point, Dr. Dio Lewis. in his excellent work on " Chastity," quotes from a report of the Massachusetts State Board of Charities as follows: " In whatever form the appetite for stimulus is indulged, whether rum, gin, wine, cider, or beer, the *alcoholic basis is the thing sought for,* and its effects are about the same in whatever form it is disguised and made palatable. Physiologists are becoming more and more unanimous in the belief that it can never give real strength or promote health. As a stimulus, it acts merely as a whip does upon a horse's skin, quickening without strengthening him. Its persistent use always tends to vitiate the system, so that for the rest of his life the person is less able than he otherwise would be to perform his social duties and contribute his proper share to the general prosperity.

"When his bodily system is once vitiated, there comes in the law of hereditary descent, so that his progeny starts in life with tainted blood, and with an appetite liable to break out into fierce passion at the first temptation.

"In order to see the connection between habitual intoxication, whether slight or severe, and subsequent insanity, or mental inability, we have only to consider that the brain is the immediate organ by which the mind acts, and that it is a compound organ, the different parts of which seem to be connected with different mental faculties, uniformity of action among them being essential to soundness of mind, or sanity. The uniform and necessary consequence of alcohol in the stomach is to excite the different parts of the brain unequally, and to produce discord where there should be harmony. This disturbance varies from slight and pleasant excitement, during which one is mirthful, to downright drunkenness, when one is savage.''

"Now it appears that during each and every one of these states of cerebral excitement, certain sub-organs of the brain are disturbed. They work inharmoniously, consequently mental equilibrium is lost. The man is, for the time, more or less insane, or unsound of mind, and so continues until the effect of the stimulus upon the nervous system ceases, and soberness, or sanity, is re-established. But gradually habit becomes law, and repetition of the stimulus seems necessary. Now, each and every disturbance of the brain impairs its perfectness as an organ. Habitual disturbance begets a chronic disturbance, which tends to become organic disease. Very soon, therefore, the organic condition of the brain gets to be permanently vitiated, so that the man does not become perfectly sane, even after he becomes sober. Organic imperfections unfit the brain for sane action, and habit confirms the insane condition— the man's brain has become unsound. Then comes in the law of hereditary descent, by which the brain of a man's child is fashioned after his own—not as it was originally, but as it has become in consequence of frequent functional disturbance. Hence, of all the appetites, the inherited appetite for drunkenness is the most direful. Natural laws contemplate no exceptions, and sins against them are never pardoned."

A writer in the *Psychological Journal* says: "The most startling problem connected with intemperance is that not only does it affect the morals, health, and intelligence of the offspring of its votaries, but they also inherit the fatal tendency and feel a craving for the very beverages which have acted as poisons on their systems from the commencement of their being."

The hope of future generations is in the personal purity of parents. If a father would have strong boys, noble of character and manly to a fault, he must forever abstain from intoxicants. Lamar-

tine truthfully says that "in the blood
of ancestry may be found the prophecy of
destiny." Parents have it in their power
to endow their children with strong
bodies and pure minds. There is a world
of truth in the old saying, " It runs in the
family." A drunkard's boy usually
drinks sooner or later. The great characters of history were not born of parents
whose bodies and minds were vitiated
from protracted dissipation. The man
who gives himself over to liquor, therefore,
is an enemy both to himself and to his
offspring, even "unto the third and fourth
generations," by which time his family
will probably have become extinct.

So much on the physical and mental
phases of the subject. Much more might
be written, but I trust this is enough to
awaken every reader to a sense of his
danger if he becomes a devotee of the
bottle. I believe that intemperance
gradually becomes a disease and with
hundreds of poor fellows all the moral
suasion of the nations would not avail in
their redemption from the power of the
demon. In such event, some kind friends,
if they have any, should barrel them

up and express them to the Keeley insti-
tute for inebriates, or some other place
where they can receive the benefits of
scientific treatment. But of the many
thousands who will read these pages,
there will probably be few, if any, who
are so completely under bondage as that,
but they should *stop* and STOP NOW! Exercise the will before it is too weak to
govern.

I would array rum against the personal
welfare of men, second, because it is a
most prolific source of financial embarrass-
ment and ruin.

Gov. St. John, in a recent address, asserts that the people of the United States
spend $1,500,000,000 for strong drink.
Think of that! Endeavor to comprehend
it! Fifteen hundred millions every fifty-
two weeks for that which is infinitely worse
than nothing! More than enough to
pay our public debt! It would be far
wiser every way if those who spend this
vast sum for liquor would put the amount
in their stoves rather than in the tills of
their saloon-keepers. For eminent authorities declare that intemperance causes
three-fourths of the crimes of our coun-

try.   Hence, we must spend oceans of
money in building prisons and reforma-
tories, maintaining courts, supporting
officers of the law, etc., most of which
would be uncalled for but for the accursed
power of strong drink.

Political orators wax eloquent and saw
the air vehemently over the tariff question every campaign.   I would not deny
the importance of the tariff question, but
would insist that the liquor problem is
one of vastly greater proportions.   Close
the drinking places of our land one year,
and use the fifteen hundred millions of dollars thus saved in building homes for the
homeless, buying clothes for the ragged,
supplying books and schools for the ignorant, food for the hungry, nurses for
the sick, and help for the needy generally,
and the experiment would work a glorious
revolution in public sentiment in favor of
teetotalism, for it is safe to say that the
condition of our people, physically, mentally, financially, and every other way,
would be improved many fold.

Why is it that the American people are
so paradoxical?   We pride ourselves in
political and religious freedom, in the

equality of men, in the maintenance of a splendid educational system, and, in short, in everything that tends to a higher development. And yet we foster this damnable traffic, which is the natural enemy and unrelenting antagonist of everything good! Is this becoming to a great *Christian* nation? Is it policy? Is it right?

If some powerful fiend from an unknown world should fly across our land to-night, torch in hand and malice in heart, and set fire to every university, college, and public school between Maine and California, and illuminate the heavens with their flames and thicken the air with their ashes—burn every one to the ground— we would consider it by far the most direful calamity that ever befell the American republic. But our liquor bill for fifty-two weeks, statisticians say, would restore every institution of learning in its original worth! ·

There are, perhaps, one million tramps in our country, men who drift about from one locality to another, working a little now and then, and begging more. Nearly all of these fellows use strong drink when

they can get it.   They often spend their
charities for beer in preference to bread.
Close the saloons, and in three months
the vast majority of this dangerous class
would quit tramping and settle down in
some decent and profitable occupation.

Prince Leopold, Duke of Albany, declared that drink was the only enemy
England had to fear.   And as long ago as
1831, when the liquor business had not
been reduced to such scientifically satanic
principles as it is to-day, Mr. Livesey
said: "While drinking continues, poverty
and vice will prevail.   And until this is
abandoned, no regulations, no efforts, no
authority under heaven, can raise the condition of the working classes.   It is worse
than a plague or a pestilence, and the
man is no friend of his country who does
not lift up his voice and proclaim his example against it."

The London *Times*, one of the leading
dailies of the world, says: "The use of
strong drink produces more idleness,
crime, want, and misery, than all other
causes put together."   Gov. Dix, of New
York, says: "Intemperance is the un-
doubted cause of four-fifths of all the

crime, pauperism, and domestic misery
of the state." And Senator Windom
says: "I do not overstate it when I say
that the two hundred thousand saloons in this country have been instru-
mental in destroying more human lives,
in the last five years, than the two millions of armed men did during the four
years of the rebellion. Whisky is a more
deadly weapon than shot and shell, or any
of the implements of our improved modern warfare."

In the third place, I would stigmatize
strong drink as the sworn enemy of man,
because it perverts his moral nature
and damns his soul. Very little
argument is necessary on this point.
Solomon said: "Wine is a mocker,
strong drink is raging; and whosoever
is deceived thereby is not wise." The
great apostle Paul goes much farther,
and declares that no drunkard shall be
permitted to inherit the kingdom of God.
(1 Cor. 6: 9, 10.) The Word of God, from
beginning to end, is clearly and emphatically against the use of strong drink.
That's enough for me. What God condemns I do not care to try to support, es-

pecially when the most advanced science of the world agrees with the Divine condemnation. Strong drink rottens every moral fibre of the being, and hastens on the awful sentence of eternal doom.

"Men and women stand before the republic to-day," says J. Howard Moore, the brilliant young temperance agitator, in a recent article, " and pencil the cost of drink. They paint the Niagara of dollars that month after month and year after year leaps into the great black maw of appetite.

"They compare it with the banks. They tell how in just nine months the whole banking capital of this country would be swept down this bottomless vortex. They show how the value of all the mines would be swallowed up in little over a twelvemonth. How the mills and factories would go in four months, and the telegraphs in five. They picture shivering, starving thousands, thronging great cities, whose principal industry is the manufacture and barter of alcoholic flames. They tell how poverty and unrest prowl the land and caterwaul in the dark places of the republic, while $2,500,000

every day from January to December is
burned up in worse than beastly lusts.

"Thousands of such scorching truths
pour incessantly from platform and pen,
until it seems the syllables would blister
on the frozen consciences of the people of
this country. Yet, men look at the fester-
ing Diabolus, pinch their nostrils, and,
like the Levite of old, pass by on the
other side.

"But, appalling as they are, the finances
of the rum scourge are infinitesimal! If
you would count the cost of rum, look not
to the cash balance alone, for money is
filth compared with the dearest interests
of human existence. Consider the woful
train that follows this frightful outlay, if
you would find its hideous total. With one
hand the liquor business steals its millions
from the pockets of poverty; with the
other it sows its myriad woes. It ruins
character, engenders vices of deepest dye,
desolates homes, blights youth in its
promise and woman's innocence, wrecks
body and brain, crowds prisons, peoples
poor-houses and mad-asylums, demor-
alizes the ballot, bribes justice and legis-
lation, breeds riots, assassinates law,

poisons and debauches society—what has the abomination *not* done? It has been indicted for every offense in crime's black catalogue, and convicted on every count.

"Sum up multiplied villainies! Count the cost of a human tear as it scalds down the cheek of agony, and multiply it by rivers! Count the cost of ruined homes and lives laid waste, multiply them by myriads and these into centuries! Count the cost of eternity in hell, and multiply it by millions!

"Go ask the wife whose husband has squandered all in the saloon, as she sits to-day wailing among the weeds of disappointment—ask her what rum has cost! Ask the mother whose darling son has fallen victim to rum's enticement, and instead of her once promising boy she beholds a besotted fiend, groveling in the gutter—ask her the cost of rum in the gilded mockery of trade! Ask the widow, as she sits with streaming eyes at the close of a blasted life and mourns for the days of happy girlhood! Ask the orphan that shivers and sobs on the stranger's door-stone! Ask the maniac, as he mut-

ters in delirious hopelessness of the days
when he was free! Ask the drunkard!
Yes, ask the inebriate what rum has cost!
Ask him in the reflective calm of soberness, when penitence claws at his conscience. Ask him as he sits amid the desolation of a drunkard's doom, looks back
over a blasted life and mourns for the
might-have-been. Ask him on the couch
of delirium tremens, when suspicion
quivers 'long every nerve. See him on
that bed of torment with kindled hell in
his soul! See him as he writhes and
groans and grapples in his death agony!
What slimy shapes crawl o'er his fevered
limbs, or gibe at him from the blue corners of his chamber! What ghastly forebodings dance in the haunted hollows of
his soul! What storms of horror rage
along his imagination! What pangs shoot
every sensory! What fiends stand by his
midnight pillow! Oh, if there is one
thing on the wide earth that will freeze
the blood in its hot cells, it is the mad
inebriate in the last throes of dissolution.

"Would you find death in all its hide-
ousness? Would you seek a life going
out amid the most excruciating woe? Go

not to the culprit as he stands on the gal-
lows under the pall of guilt, and, with his
eyes scanning the parapets of eternity,
contemplates death. Go not to Sappho
with her heart scorching with rejected
love as she drowns her affection in the
Ionian waters. Go not to Napoleon, standing lone and pensive on St. Helena, gazing
above the tossing strand toward sunny
France. But if you would find death in all
its unmitigated woe, go to the hovel—go
to the home of the drunkard—stand by the
bedside of the dying inebriate as the last
rays of mortality fade—see that life,
whose morning perhaps was roseate with
promise, slowly ebbing away into night,
dark and starless as Stygian gloom. No
hopes gladden his miserable exit! No
blessings girdle his contorted brow! No
vigils mourn the flickering of his dying
heart-throbs! No requiem he, but widows' wails and orphans' woes rising in
hopeless lamentations to the Eternal
Throne!

"Count the cost of rum if you would—
yes, count it if you can—but count it not
in the mockery of dollars!"

O, men, as you value your present and

eternal felicity, I implore you to "touch
not, taste not, handle not" strong drink!
Keep yourselves pure from the accursed
stuff. And do not support its manufacture or sale in any way. Use voice and
vote against it. Fight the wicked business with all your might. I have little
patience with any man who professes to
be a Christian and yet votes a license
ticket. It is utterly inconsistent. If
you are a praying man, *vote as you pray*.
The average saloon-keeper fears one active ballot more than a dozen passive
prayers. If all professed followers of
Christ would *work just as hard as they
pray*, and *pray just as hard as they work*,
we could close every liquor shop in America within eighteen months.

"Intemperance cuts down youth in its
vigor, manhood in its strength, and age
in its weakness. It breaks the father's
heart, bereaves the doting mother, extin-
guishes natural affections, erases conjugal
love, blots out filial attachments, and
blasts parental hopes, and brings down
mourning age in sorrow to the grave. It
produces weakness, not strength; sickness, not health; death, not life. It

makes wives, widows; children, orphans; fathers, fiends—and all of them paupers and beggars. It feeds rheumatism, nurses gout, welcomes epidemics, invites cholera, imparts pestilence and embraces consumption. It covers the land with idleness, misery and crime. It fills your jails, supplies your almshouses and demands your asylums. It engenders controversies, fosters quarrels and cherishes riots. It crowds your penitentiaries, and furnishes victims to your scaffolds. It is the life-blood of the gambler, the element of the burglar, the prop of the highwayman, and the support of the midnight incendiary. It countenances the liar, respects the thief, esteems the blasphemer. It violates obligations, reverences fraud, honors infamy. It defames benevolence, hates love, scorns virtue, and slanders innocence. It incites the father to butcher his helpless offspring; helps the husband to massacre his wife, and the child to grind the parracidal axe. It burns up men, consumes women, detests life, curses God and despises Heaven. It suborns witnesses, nurses **perjury**, defiles the jurybox, and stains the judicial er-

mine. It degrades the citizen, debases
the legislature, dishonors the statesman,
and disarms the patriot. It brings shame,
not honor; terror, not safety; despair, not
hope; misery, not happiness; and with
the malevolence of a fiend, it calmly sur-
veys its frightful desolation—and, unsat-
isfied with its havoc, it poisons felicity,
kills peace, ruins morals, blights confidence, slays reputation, and wipes out
national honor; then curses the world
and laughs at its ruin. It does all that
and more—it murders the soul! It is the
sum of all villainies, the father of all
crimes, the mother of all abomination, the
devil's best friend, and God's worst
enemy."

If you are a drinking man, quit at once.
Never swallow another drop. You can't
be a pure man and continue the use of
strong drink. All the arguments are
against it. Seventy thousand poor fellows in this country kill themselves with
strong drink every year, and bring a
legion of miseries upon their poor fam-
iles. Truly, as a current writer says of
the rum traffic, "it wades through rivers
of blistering tears which it forces from

tender hearts to produce eighty per cent. of all our crime." It is estimated that three thousand wives perished under the cruelty of drunken husbands in 1891. It is high time for a general uprising of public sentiment. But all reforms must begin with the individual. So once more, let me beg of every reader of these lines, shun strong drink. It is emphatically *the devil in liquid form.*

I will close this chapter with President Simpson Ely's celebrated "Impeachment of King Alcohol:"

I impeach King Alcohol because he destroys the health.

I impeach him because he disfigures the body.

I impeach him because he ruins the nervous system.

I impeach him because he dethrones reason and is the fruitful cause of idiocy and insanity.

I impeach him because he blunts the finer feelings and sensibilities of the soul.

I impeach him because he destroys every principle of manhood.

I impeach him because he destroys both soul and body in hell.

I impeach him because he would depopulate heaven and people hell.

I impeach him because he squanders property and produces pauperism.

I impeach him because he crowds our poor-houses.

I impeach him because he costs this nation every year over $900,000,000.

I impeach him because Wm. E. Gladstone, Premier of England, says he costs England year after year more than war, pestilence and famine combined.

I impeach him because he squanders paint. He paints houses too little and noses too much. Those who paint their noses most paint their houses least.

I impeach him because he murdered Alexander the Great, Stephen A. Douglas and Richard Yates.

I impeach him because he planted a saloon in the basement of our Capitol at Washington and thus debauches our National Senators and Representatives.

I impeach him because he has corrupted our courts, defied justice, ignored law and perjured witnesses.

I impeach him because he has shadowed

homes, broken hearts and beggared innocent wives and children.

I impeach him because he leads to three-
fourths of the litigations in our courts.

I impeach him because he leads his subjects into violence, murder, and every
conceivable crime.

I impeach the United States Government because it is in partnership with
King Alcohol.

I impeach all brewers, distillers, saloon-
ists and druggists who are the mercenary
abettors of his majesty, King Alcohol.

I impeach those who vote for license,
support whisky men, sign drug store and
saloon petitions, oppose prohibition or
remain silent on this question.   These all
are the supporters of King Alcohol.   They
are *particeps criminis.*

What is the remedy?   TOTAL ABSTI-
NENCE FOR THE INDIVIDUAL, PROHIBITION FOR
THE STATE.

CHAPTER IV.

TOBACCO; OR, HEATHENDOM'S MOST POPULAR GIFT TO CHRISTENDOM.

Tobacco is one of the most fruitful causes of degeneracy in our nineteenth century manhood. It is heathendom's most popular gift to Christendom. Millions use the "weed"—old men and young, saints and sinners, learned and unlearned, in short, all classes and conditions of human society have been victimized by this unhallowed pest.

I am aware that he who opposes the use of tobacco tramps on many toes. The habit is one of the most common evils of the age. At Johnstown, Pa., I once lectured to men only. Over one thousand were present. When I put the question, How many of you use tobacco in some form? about nine hundred hands went up. Many seemed ashamed to own it, but when urged to be honest in the matter, were compelled to admit their guilt. It is so almost everywhere. The evil is one of tremendous proportions, and I think it is high time every lover of personal purity were taking a stand against it. Happily, the tobacco habit is confined almost exclusively to the sterner sex. Few females use tobacco.

"The origin of a custom which has enslaved many millions of human beings in its toils," says Dr. Kellogg in one of his well-known "Health Science Leaflets," "which has within a few centuries fixed itself so firmly upon the race, and become so wide-spread as to be practically universal among mankind, whether civilized or savage, cannot be without interest to those who are users of the weed, as well as to those who wage war against this evil practice. The latter, especially, will find in the ignoble origin of tobacco-using an argument of no little force against this vile habit."

"In the month of November, 1492, when Columbus discovered the island of Cuba, he sent two sailors to explore it, who reported, when they returned, among many other strange and curious discoveries, that the natives carried with them lighted fire-brands, and puffed smoke from their mouths and noses, which they supposed to be the way the savages had of perfuming themselves! They afterwards declared that they saw the naked savages twist large leaves together and 'smoke like devils.'

"To civilized human beings this was the first sight of the vile habit which has become so common that every city, town, and village is actually perfumed, or, more properly, befouled, with the vile stench of the poisonous weed. The impression made upon the unsophisticated Europeans was evidently not greatly in favor of the custom, since they compared the smoking Indians to devils. Originating with the wild barbarians of America, the smoking habit was after some years introduced into Europe, and receiving the sanction of physicians, who just at that time chiefly occupied themselves in searching for new nauseous compounds with which to experiment upon the lives of their patients, it was rapidly adopted, not only by the lower classes, but by those in high authority, even princes and nobles participating in the new intoxication.

" It appears that the taking of tobacco in the form of snuff was also discovered among the savage natives of this continent upon the second visit of Columbus to America, in 1494. A Roman friar, named Pane, who accompanied the expedition, thus describes the custom as it then existed among the Indians: 'After reducing the leaves to a fine powder, they take it through a cane half a cubit long. One end of this they place in the nose and the other upon the powder, and so draw it up, which purges them much.' The purging referred to evidently describes the violent sneezing which resulted from the inhalation of the powdered poison. If the sailors thought that the smoking savages appeared ' like devils,' they certainly must have been ready to compare a party of sneezing Indians to a group of lunatics. How so filthy, unnatural, and eminently disgusting a habit could ever have been cultivated by rational beings, is a most profound mystery.

" In 1503, when the Spaniards landed in Paraguay, the natives attempted to repulse them, and came out against them in large numbers, beating drums, throwing water, and 'chewing herbs and spurting juice toward them.' The herb employed was tobacco, and the object of its use in the peculiar manner indicated was to get the poisonous juice into the eyes of the intruders and thus disable them by depriving them of sight. From this it would seem that tobacco-chewing was first practiced as a means of defense, for which purpose the expectorated juice was undoubtedly quite effective. We have seen modern tobacco-chewers whose copious expectoration made it next to impossible for any one to approach within several feet without being soiled by the juice. In the days when warfare was carried on by hand-to-hand combat, we can very readily understand that a wild Indian, filling the air about him in all directions with poisonous, irritating, filthy tobacco juice, would be a very formidable object.

"The first smokers employed what was practically identical with the modern cigar. Dry tobacco leaves were made into rolls and wrapped with the leaves of Indian corn, one end being lighted, and

the other placed in the mouth. Pipes
were also employed, those used in North
America being shaped almost exactly like
the letter Y, except that the stem was
longer and the forked end was symmet-
rical. In use, the forked end was placed
in the nostrils, and the other end in the
dense smoke arising from tobacco leaves
placed on glowing coals. In Mexico and
South America, pipes almost precisely
like those now in use, with numerous
other forms, were employed in the same
way in which pipes are now used.

"Thus it appears that tobacco-using,
together with the implements of its use
and all the different modes of taking it,
originated wholly with the heathen barbarians who roamed like wild beasts over
the plains and through the dense forests
of this continent four centuries ago. Civilized men have made no improvements
or discoveries of any account in connection with its use; they have simply followed the example of these naked savages
whom the discoverers of America saw
chewing, snuffing, and smoking 'like
devils' four hundred years ago. It is
evident, then, that tobacco-using is a

barbarous custom in the fullest sense.
As to how savages learned the use of the
weed, history does not give us any hint;
but the fact that pipes and snuff-taking
tubes are found in their most ancient
burial mounds, which are often sur-
mounted by huge trees that must have
required many centuries for their growth,
is evidence of its great antiquity; and in
this habit we may unquestionably find
one of the causes which have reduced the
American savage to his present degraded
and deteriorated condition."

But what if it is of heathen origin?
says some victim of the habit. Why
fight it so bitterly? Why be over-senti-
mental about it?

It is not merely a matter of sentiment,
dear friend. It is a matter of grave con-
cern from various standpoints. Dr. John
Ellis, in his "New Christianity," says
that he is "more and more impressed with
the conviction that tobacco is doing more
towards sapping the physical constitution
of the American people than even alcoholic
drinks. Its effects are more insidious, and
comparatively unperceived by the popular eye, and even by the victim himself;

therefore destruction is more certain and irresistible. Then again the habit is quite as strong and as difficult to break as the habit of using alcoholic drinks, and therefore it makes its votaries no less abject slaves. One of the most notorious drunkards we have ever known, who was also in the habit of using tobacco, assured the writer that he would much sooner be without his whisky than his tobacco, that his sufferings and cravings were less. Such, we think, will generally be found to be the testimony of those who have come fully under the dominion of both habits."

I am against tobacco, in the first place, because it is poisonous. "Chemists, botanists, and physicians," says Dr. Kellogg, " unite in pronouncing tobacco one of the most deadly poisons known. No other poison, with the exception of prussic acid, will cause death so quickly, only three or four minutes being required for a fatal dose to produce its full effect. It is botanically known as *nicotiana tabacum,* and belongs to a class of plants known as the *volanaceæ*, which includes the most poisonous of all species of plants,

among which are henbane and belladonna.
There are more than forty different
varieties of the plant, all of which possess
the same general properties, though
varying in the degree of poisonous
character. The active principle of tobacco, that is that to which its narcotic
and poisonous properties are due, is nicotine, a heavy, oily substance, which may
be separated from the dried leaf of the
plant by distillation or infusion. The
proportion of nicotine varies from two to
eight per cent., Kentucky and Virginia
tobacco usually containing six or seven
per cent. A pound of tobacco contains,
on an average, three hundred and eighty
grains of this deadly poison, of which one-
tenth of a grain will kill a dog in ten
minutes. A case is on record in which
a man was killed in thirty seconds by this
poison.

"The poison contained in a single
pound of tobacco is sufficient to kill three
hundred men, if taken in such a way as
to secure its full effect. A single cigar
contains poison enough to extinguish
two human lives, if taken at once. The
essential oil has been used for homicidal

purposes. Nearly thirty years ago, it was employed by the Count Bocarme to murder his brother-in-law, for the purpose of securing his property. Hottentots use the oil of tobacco to kill snakes, a single minute drop causing death as quickly as a lightning stroke. It is much used by gardeners and keepers of greenhouses to destroy grubs and noxious insects. A number of instances are recorded in which death has been produced by applying a little of the oil from the stem or bowl of an old pipe to a sore upon the head or face of a small child."

" One of the most prevalent of bad habits," said Dr. Foote, in his " Plain Home Talk," years ago, " is the use of tobacco. This poisonous weed is extensively used by nearly every community under the sun. In New York City alone, there are about 200,000 smokers, and nearly as many chewers of tobacco, to say nothing of snuff-takers. It is estimated that its citizens spend daily over $10,000 for cigars, and less than $9,000 for bread. The Europeans, and the present white inhabitants of the continent, borrowed the habit of smoking of the aborigines of

America, and the Asiatics somehow or other got hold of the trick themselves. Many fashionable ladies on both sides of the Atlantic smoke their cigarettes, and a cigar dealer in Boston makes the astounding announcement that he sells an average of three hundred *cigars* daily for the use of the fair ones of New England. According to Johnson, every female in the big empire of China, from the age of eight or nine years, wears as an appendage in her dress a small silken pocket to hold tobacco and a pipe. The Japanese also smoke, women as well as men. A majority of men all over the world smoke or chew, and not a few boys follow their illustrious (!) example. The poet Milton was a moderate smoker, and Lamb at one time carried smoking to a great excess. The latter in a letter to Wordsworth said, 'Tobacco has been my evening comfort and morning curse for these five years.' The great preacher Robert Hall claimed to have adopted the habit of smoking to qualify himself for the society of a certain doctor of divinity (!), and finally he became such a slave to it that he found himself unable to overcome it." After a very interesting discussion of the subject, Dr. Foote says, "The long and short of the whole matter is this: tobacco is a medicinal plant, just as much so as belladonna, stramonium, hyoscyamus, etc., all of which belong to the same order, and should not be indulged in by healthy people any more than cathartics and emetics. Its habitual use by healthy people is attended by injury to the nerves and blood."

"That tobacco is a poison," says Dr. Ellis, "will be questioned by no one who has seen the deadly sickness which a very small dose will cause in a person not habituated to its use—even smoking part of a cigar, or chewing for a few moments a small portion. *In fact, tobacco is one of the most virulent poisons in nature.* It seems to act not only upon the brain and spinal cord, but also especially upon the great sympathetic system of nerves, which is the very citadel of life."

"Dr. Brodie, a celebrated English physician, applied a single drop of the oil of tobacco to the tongue of a cat, upon which bodily prostration and convulsions ensued. Another drop applied, and the

animal died in two minutes. One drop
injected into the rectum of a cat occa-
sioned death in about five minutes; and
two drops administered in the same
manner to a dog was followed by the
same result.   Dr. Franklin applied the
oily material which floats on the surface of water when a current of tobacco
smoke is passed into it, to the tongue of a
cat, and found it to destroy life in a few
minutes; yet the cat is more tenacious
of life than almost any other animal."

   " We regard tobacco," says Dr. Potter,
" as one of the greatest enemies of the
human family, and indeed of all life.
* * * Dr. Dixon very properly main-
tains that the use of tobacco, in any shape,
is productive of the most fearful physical
results. He attributes, in fact, most of the
distressing maladies we are subject to, as
well as the gaunt, sallow countenances of
too many Americans, to the nicotine, or
oil of tobacco, infused into the system by
the general habit of smoking or chewing.
' Nicotine,' remarks this able physician,
' was the awful agent chosen by Bocarme
for poisoning his brother-in-law, because
it killed and left no sign whereby to con-

vict him.' He adds that 'five drops of
the oil of tobacco will kill a large dog.' "

Dr. Coles declares that " a single leaf,
dipped in hot water and laid upon the pit
of the stomach, will produce a powerful
effect by mere absorption from the surface. By being applied to a spot where
the scarf skin, or external surface of the
skin, is destroyed, fearful results have followed."

Now what must be the logical result of
using tobacco? It causes a multitude of
diseases, dulls the mental faculties, and
hastens death. In this scientists are
agreed. "The fact is established beyond
the possibility of successful controversy,"
says Dr. Kellogg, "that tobacco is a poison, deadly in large doses, pernicious and
harmful in all doses. It taints the breath,
ruins the digestion, obliterates taste and
smell, spoils the blood, oppresses the
brain, depresses the heart, irritates the
nerves, wastes the muscles, obstructs the
liver, dims the vision, stains the skin, and
deteriorates and contaminates every organ
and tissue with which it comes in contact
in the body. Its influence is to lessen

vitality, to benumb the sensibilities, to shorten life, *to kill.*"

"It is often objected that while chemistry and scientific experiments seem to prove that tobacco is a powerful poison, the experience of thousands of persons disproves the theory of its poisonous character, since, if it were so intense a poison as described, cases of death from tobacco-poisoning would be much more frequent. To this objection, we answer: 1. One reason why so few persons are reputed to die of *nicotine,* or tobacco-poisoning, is the wonderful faculty the system possesses of accommodating itself to circumstances. Through this means, the worst poisons may by degrees be tolerated, until enormous doses can be taken without immediately fatal effects. Corrosive sublimate, strychnia, belladonna, and many other poisons may be thus tolerated. 2. In our opinion, the majority of tobacco-users do die of tobacco-poisoning. Death as surely results, ultimately, from chronic as from acute poisoning, though the full effects are delayed, it may be, for years. A man who died five or ten years sooner than he should, in consequence of tobacco-using, is killed by the poison just as truly as though he died instantly from an overdose."

Mr. Barrow, the African traveler, gives us the following interesting and instructive description of the way some of the inhabitants of the dark continent dispose of snakes: "A Hottentot applied some of it (tobacco-poison) from the short end of his wooden pipe to the mouth of a snake while darting out his tongue. The effect was as instantaneous as that of an electric shock. With a momentary convulsive motion, the snake half twisted itself, and never stirred more. Its muscles were so contracted that the whole animal felt as hard and rigid as if dried in the sun."

Prof. Silliman somewhere gives an account of a Yale student who cut his life short by indulging in the use of this poison. "He entered," says the Professor, "with an athletic frame; but he acquired the habit of using tobacco, and would sit and smoke whole hours together. His friends tried to persuade him to quit the practice, but he loved his lust, and would have it, live or die—the consequence of

which was he went down to the grave a
suicide."

One writer declares that "there is infinitely more poison in one package of tobacco, than in the tin foil that surrounds
hundreds."

Tobacco is a very potent cause of disease. Its constant use lowers the vital
tone of the system, and thus predisposes
to various ailments, among which may be
mentioned the following:

(1) *Nervousness.* "Every narcotic," says
Dr. Kellogg, "has the effect to diminish
the nerve tone, and it is only a question
of time when the nerve tone will become
exhausted, and then the individual will
become a victim of that hydra-headed
malady, neurasthenia, or nervous debility." Take away from a tobacco-user
his "plug" or pipe, and see how restless
and peevish he will soon become. His
appetite, long abused, craves the poisonous stimulant, and, unless satisfied,
promptly creates such a general disturbance as to make the victim and all his as-
sociates very uncomfortable. "Tobacco
is the fruitful cause of nervousness, and
not its cure," says President Ely. "Per-

haps those who use it act upon the old saying that 'the hair of the dog will cure its bite.' Like alcohol, tobacco is a stimulant; but it is an unnatural stimulant, and foreign to our natures, and all such are very injurious to the human system. They may 'brace you up'; but the reaction and depression are sure to follow; and if the slave to tobacco lives to see his three score years and ten, he is generally so nervous that he can scarcely lift a cup of water to his lips, and it is difficult for him to spit beyond his shirt front. And what a spectacle is this! In Iowa, I knew an excellent old gentleman in many respects; but he was almost helpless because of nervousness, and when I asked him the cause, he answered at once, 'It is tobacco.' And he further said, 'I would freely give a thousand dollars if I could be free from this habit.' He was wealthy, and doubtless meant every word that he said. What a blessed consummation if the boys and young men could all be induced to spare themselves such servitude to this worse than useless practice, and thus escape such

vain regrets as that old man expressed.
Avoid nervousness by avoiding tobacco."

(2) *Dyspepsia, Paralysis, etc.* "Tobacco is a frequent cause of dyspepsia,"
says Dr. Ellis. "It occasions spasmodic
pressure of the stomach; heartburn; feeling of coldness of the stomach; nausea,
and frequent eructations; pains in the region of the liver, and diseases of that organ;
gan; pains in the bowels, with disposition
to diarrhœa or costiveness. It produces
difficulty of breathing, oppression and
pains in the chest, with inability to take
in a long breath, and violent palpitation
of the heart. It causes pain and stiffness
of the back. Tobacco also creates a tendency to paralysis, both general and local.
It gives rise to drowsiness, unnatural
sleep, nightmare, troublesome, anxious
and frightful dreams, together with a
great variety of symptoms which we have
not space to notice. In fact, we have described but a small share of the symptoms
and diseases which are noticed by our
best medical writers and most careful observers as having been brought on or
aggravated by the use of this poison. Not
that it will cause all of these symptoms

in any one person, for it affects different individuals differently, manifesting its action in the weak organs, or upon the parts of the body which are least able to resist its influence. But there is no one who uses tobacco who will not find himself troubled with more or less of these symptoms the very moment he quits using the poison; but while he is using it freely, it will palliate, as do all poisons, the symptoms its habitual use has caused. In the morning, after having abstained during the night, the tobacco-user will get a glimpse of his waning vital energies, but his view will soon be covered over by the oblivious leaves of the demon when he again partakes."

(3) *A stunted growth.* The same writer says he was "never more painfully conscious of the terrible effects of the habitual use of tobacco than during a visit to a locality where reside many of the friends of his childhood and youth. He found a large number of the gentlemen, the sons of robust parents, addicted to its use, and its effects were to be seen in every lineament of their countenances—emaciated, prematurely wrinkled, and sallow; look-

ing, in fact, almost as much like wilted
tobacco leaves as like human beings in
the full pride of manhood. But he found
two gentlemen who had used tobacco for
many years formerly (and when last seen
they were suffering excessively from its
use), but they had given it up and were
looking like new creatures. They were
better in flesh, better in spirits, and free
from a multitude of aches and pains which
had formerly tormented them."

Thoughtful observers everywhere declare that the use of tobacco retards both
the physical and mental development if
begun before maturity. So prevalent is
this theory, that several European countries, and several of our own States, have
by statutory enactment prohibited the
sale of tobacco to boys. Rev. Wayland,
in a letter from Cuba to the *National
Baptist*, speaking of the excessive use of
tobacco in that country, says: "The
effect of this indulgence is apparent to
the most careless observer; the race is
dwindling, mind and body. Several
Cubans confessed to me that this was the
prime cause of the general degeneration
of the human species in the island." It

is said that in Switzerland and Spain tobacco is almost universally used. It is a
fact well known that the inhabitants of
these countries are neither physically nor
intellectually what they ought to be, considering their natural advantages and
age. Tobacco has stunted their growth;
and it is doing the same for Americans,
though in a less marked degree, because
not so generally used.

(4) *Consumption.* The constant breathing into the lungs of nicotinized air on
the part of smokers is a terribly prolific
cause of lung disease. In this distinguished sanitarians are agreed. Dr. Drysdale, chief physician to the Metropolitan
Free Hospital of London, says that
"smoking in youth is no uncommon
cause of pulmonary consumption."

(5) *Smoker's cancer, heart disease, tobacco blindness, etc.* "All eminent sur-
geons," says Dr. Kellogg, "testify that
they frequently meet cases of cancer of
the lips and tongue which have been oc-
casioned by smoking." "The death of
Gen. Grant and several other prominent
public men within the last few years from
smoker's cancer has fully informed the

public of the fact that the filthy weed is
capable of inducing this horrible and usually incurable malady."

Various forms of heart disease, affections of the ocular and olfactory senses, etc.,
are frequently brought on by the excessive use of tobacco. The man who prides
himself in a pure and healthful body had
better abstain once and for all from this
disease-breeding demon. Its use will do
you no good, and may injure you incal-
culably. Benjamin Franklin said: "I
never saw a well man in the exercise of
common sense who would say that tobacco did him any good."

It is said that no student who used tobacco has graduated with honors from
Harvard in the past fifty years. Tobacco
dulls the mind. President Ely, in his
"Ten Chapters Against Tobacco," gives
us the following pregnant paragraph:
"Prof. Homer Seerly, President of the
Educational Association of Iowa, and a
long time Principal of the Public Schools
of Oskaloosa, published an address to parents, in which he stated that the boys
who used tobacco might almost as well
be kept out of school. He said the to-

bacco habit unfitted them for diligent study and close application. Everywhere evil report clings to the habit, and none are more free to condemn it than those who use it."

Dr. Richardson, one of the highest medical and scientific authorities of England, says: "I do not hesitate to say that if a community of both sexes whose progenitors were finely formed and powerful were to be trained to the early practice of smoking, and if marriage were confined to the smokers, an apparently new and inferior race of men and women would be bred up."

"So closely is the nature of licentiousness interwoven with that of alcoholic liquors, opium, and tobacco," says Dr. John Cowan, "that it is difficult to tell which depends upon the other for its stimulus. But be that as it may, it is required as an absolute necessity that the individual give up the use of tobacco in all its forms, and ale, wine, whisky, cider, and all other alcoholic liquors; for a man cannot possibly live a chaste life, sexually or otherwise, who uses these soul-debasing articles; and if the individual cannot

or will not give up these habits, it is almost useless for him to read further. No
other two habits so blot, stain, and deform
the soul of man, made in God's own
image, as do tobacco and alcohol, and it
is useless for a man to try and live a
healthy or continent life who, in the re-
motest way, continues in their use."

Dr. Edward Smith, another eminent
English authority, speaking against the
poisonous weed, says: "Its whole tendency is toward disease, and it is impossible to say how much of good it has pre-
vented."

The celebrated Dr. Rush says: "A desire is excited by tobacco for strong
drinks, and these lead to drunkenness."
And Dr. Woodward agrees with him
when he says: "I have supposed tobacco
was the common stepping-stone to that
use of spirituous liquors which leads to
intemperance."

Dr. Prince, for many years the superintendent of the insane asylum at North-
ampton, Mass., says: "Fully half the
patients that have come to our asylum
for treatment are the victims of tobacco."

I am against tobacco, in the second

place, because it is a filthy and harmful
nuisance. Its promiscuous use is an insult
to all refinement. Whether chewed or
smoked, "it causes a constant inclination
to spit, which is regarded by all civilized nations (with the exception of Americans and tobacco-users) as a filthy and
unnecessary practice; and it adds to the
character of the saliva the juice of the
nauseous weed." Thousands of good
people, both male and female, cannot endure the smell of tobacco. It sickens
them immediately, often producing a severe headache, or other disorder. And yet
smokers of the stuff do not refrain from
filling our street cars, omnibuses, post-
offices, depots and other public places, with
its poisonous fumes, while chewers, utterly oblivious of the rights or welfare of
others, "deliberately defile themselves and
their surroundings by rolling the noxious
weed beneath their tongues, and expec-
torating its stinking juice upon the floor."
This is exercising personal liberty with a
vengeance!

"If human beings possess one inaliena-
ble right more sacred than any other,"
says Dr. Kellogg, "it is the right to

breathe the atmosphere of heaven, pure,
free, and unadulterated. No man has
any better right to puff tobacco smoke
into the air I am about to breathe than
to defile the water I am about to drink,
or to sit down beside me at the dinner
table and sprinkle upon the food I eat
vile and loathsome substances, obnoxious
to the senses and deleterious to the
health."

" Tobacco smoke is excellent in its
place. The writer set an old smoker going in a greenhouse one day with good
effect. Every living thing that was able
to travel left for parts unknown, and the
few who were not able to get away died of
nicotine poisoning—all except the smoker
himself, who was tough and nicotine-
proof. Tobacco is to be recommended to
kill vermin of all sorts, except a kind of
parasite that breeds in bar rooms and bil-
liard halls, and may often be seen adher-
ing to lamp posts, hovering around street
corners and railway stations, or paying
respects to the aboriginal smoker that
stands in effigy before the door of every
first-class tobacco emporium, inviting
these students of archeology to walk in

and repeat the experiment described by
Christopher Columbus, when he wrote in
his ship journal, ' We saw the naked savages twist huge leaves together and
smoke like devils '—not a very interesting experiment it would seem, but one
which possesses such a strange fascination that since this description by Columbus nearly one-half of the civilized world
have been following the example of these
naked savages."

In a Cincinnati street car some time
since, according to one of the daily papers
of that city, a gentleman lost his life
through this delectable custom. "He
was an occasional sufferer from heart disease, and the trouble was so aggravated
by the suffocating smoke of the car that
he died after breathing it a few minutes.
The car in which he rode had only one
compartment for men, women, and children, and the smokers were allowed full
sway in it. Two other passengers were
overcome by the tobacco fumes."

Horace Greeley, speaking of the smell of
tobacco smoke, said: "It is a profane
stench." And Daniel Webster strikingly,
if not eloquently, exclaimed: " If those

men must smoke, let them take the horse-shed!" But this is poor advice, for there is imminent danger of losing your horse-shed and all your horses! Hundreds of thousands of dollars worth of property is annually destroyed by fire through the carelessness of smokers.

I believe it was Rev. Sam Jones who spoke of the lighted cigar as "a head-light toward damnation." His past experience with the weed no doubt makes him thus severe. "Preachers," says President Ely, "are so much in the habit of preaching to others that they sometimes forget the necessity of being taught themselves. There is sometimes danger of the preacher, like the guide-post, indicating the right way, but failing to go that way himself. We must preach by example as well as precept. Consistency is nowhere a more precious jewel than in the pulpit, and preachers are sometimes shorn of their strength by the Delilah of inconsistency. There was seldom a more withering re-buke than that administered to Sam Jones in St. Louis. He was condemning theatres in unsparing terms and reached his climax by exclaiming, 'How would

Jesus Christ look in a theater?'   At the
next meeting he found on the stand the
query, 'How would Jesus look with a
quid of tobacco or a cigar in his mouth?'
During his Chicago meeting, he quit the
use of tobacco, and he can now consistently condemn the pet sins and follies of
others.   When I saw him I had never
met a worse slave to the tobacco habit."

"One reason why there are so many
victims of this habit," says a talented
writer, "is because there are so many
ministers of religion who smoke and
chew.   They smoke until they get the
bronchitis, and the dear people have to
pay their expenses to Europe.   They
smoke until the nervous system breaks
down.   They smoke themselves to death.
I could name three eminent clergymen
who died of cancer in the mouth, and in
every case the physician said it was tobacco.   There has been many a clergy-
man whose tombstone was all covered up
with eulogy, which ought to have had the
honest epitaph, 'killed by too much
cavendish.'   Some of them smoke until
the room is blue, and their spirits are
blue, and the world is blue, and every-

thing is blue. Time was when God
passed by such sins; but it becomes now
the duty of the American clergy who indulge in this narcotic to repent."

At Louisiana, Mo., I once conducted a
revival. That pretty old city boasted of
a tobacco factory which did a million
dollar business annually. A prominent
Baptist was president of the company.
My observations there convinced me, as
never before, as to the exceeding harmfulness and filthiness of tobacco. Many individuals there were living pictures of
the deplorable fact that the unsavory
weed impedes both physical and mental
development. The floor in the corner of
the church house, where most of the
young men sat during my services, was
literally plastered with filthy expecto-
rations, said plastering here and there
emphasized with a well-chewed quid.
There were some excellent people there.
But it was up-hill work to move the
masses to accept Christianity under such
unhallowed circumstances.

"We are taught to preserve the body
blameless unto the coming of our Lord
Jesus Christ," says President Ely, in one

of his striking paragraphs. "Were the Lord to come now, I fear he would find many who are not trying to obey that injunction. Were he to enter some of our church houses, he would find plenty of Christians sitting in the midst of sloughs of tobacco juice who would be compelled to run to the door and empty the filthy contents of their mouths before they could bid him welcome. I approached an old brother in the church once, just after benediction, and said, How do you do, Bro.——? In attempting to respond, he choked, and the horrible tobacco juice spurted out of his mouth and ran down his beard and shirt-front. Shades of the 'precious ointment that ran down upon the beard, even Aaron's beard: that went down to the skirts of his garment!'"

Dr. Coles, in his "Beauties and Deformities of Tobacco-using," relates the following significant anecdote. "A professor in a western college was traveling in company with a clerical brother. They stopped to spend the Lord's day, and the professor was invited to preach in the evening. His brother in the ministry,

who was a practical admirer of tobacco
and its fruits, was with him in the desk.
The professor set his hat (a new one) at
the end of the pulpit sofa; and while
preaching, he saw his brother, who was so
near-sighted that he mistook the hat for
a spit-box, delivering the contents of his
mouth every moment into his hat. But
he was obliged to submit to the process.
It would not do to make an apostrophe in
his sermon by saying, 'Don't spit your
vile stuff into my hat!' So he bore it like
a saint and let his brother spit away—
casting into his new-fashioned spittoon
not only the syrup from his powerful
tobacco-mill, but 'cud' after 'cud' of the
solid refuse. Think what a hat the professor had after the meeting was closed!"
He threw it away, and went home hatless
and unhappy.

"So nauseous is even the taste of
tobacco," writes Dr. Ellis, "that in all
the animal kingdom but two animals,
aside from man, have been discovered
which will taste it—the tobacco worm of
the south, whose intolerable visage is disgusting, and the rock goat of Africa. The
goat is thought by one writer to possess a

bodily odor which prepares it for association with those who produce in themselves the tobacco stench. The smell of
this goat is so terrible that no other
dumb animal will even associate with it.
The very atmosphere for a distance around
is tainted with his effluvia, and his whole
visage is said to be disgusting. The
tobacco-user is said to become so pickled
with tobacco that cannibals detect it in
the flesh of those who have used it, and
throw that flesh away as unfit to use. It
is immaterial how tobacco is used,
whether it be by smoking, chewing, snuffing or dipping, the effects are similar."

"Let a company spend the evening in
smoking," says Rev. Todd, in a popular
work to students, "and what is the effect?
They all awake in the morning restless,
feverish, low-spirited, and dissatisfied.
The bell grates upon the nerves worse
than ever. The mouth is clammy and bitter, the stomach uneasy, and each one feels
like pouring out the vital principle in yawn-
ing. The custom certainly seems most at
home in a filthy ale-house or bar-room. All
experienced people will tell you that the
habit of using tobacco in any shape will

soon render you emaciated and con-
sumptive, your nerves shattered, your
spirits low and moody, your throat dry,
and demanding stimulating drinks, your
person filthy, and your habits those of a
swine."

I am against tobacco in the third place
because it causes a lavish waste of money.
It requires but a few years' time to smoke
up or chew up the price of a good farm
or beautiful residence. It goes out in
small amounts, and tobacco-users do not
realize how much they waste. In comparing the liquor and tobacco habits, a
friend said to me recently, "The latter is
not so bad because it does not cause a
man to neglect and impoverish his family
like the liquor habit does." Perhaps not
quite so bad, and yet a thousand times
too much so. Let us figure a little.
Suppose a man spends fifty cents a day
for himself and his treats—the price of
only ten cigars of medium quality. This
would amount to $15 per month, or $180
per year, enough to pay the rent for a
comfortable home in an average location.
Or, if the smoker would save his fifty
cents daily and put it at interest at the

rate of six per cent., he would have over
$47,000 to his credit at the expiration of
fifty years.

I know a man in Iowa who will soon be
sixty years old. He has used tobacco about
fifty years. He is a farmer by occupation, but doesn't own a foot of land in
the world, and probably never will. He
has been a renter all these years, driven
about from pillar to post, always poor and
pleading poverty. He has worse than
wasted the price of a better farm than he
has ever lived on in his slavish devotion
to this nasty habit. He had naturally a
splendid constitution, but, like his older
brother, who is also a devotee of the weed,
he will undoubtedly "break down before
his time." There are multitudes of such
instances on every hand.

Statisticians say that the people of
the United States consume over $600,-
000,000 worth of tobacco every year.
"Every dollar is the price of iniquity,"
says President Ely. "It is an evil gain
to those who sell it, and a terrible loss to
those who consume it." Bread is rightly
called the "staff of life," and meat doubtless holds second place in the larders of

Americans. But we spend more for tobacco than we do for both bread and meat. "Put into my hand the moneys wasted in tobacco in the United States of America," says Rev. T. De Witt Talmage, "and I will clothe, feed and shelter all the suffering poor on this continent." We spend many times as much for tobacco as we do in the support of our public schools. We spend more than one hundred times as much for tobacco than for both home and foreign missions. The money the United States alone spends for tobacco would double the present missionary force of the world. We call ourselves a Christian nation, but oh, what a barbarous use of our opportunities we are making!

There are other phases of the tobacco question which I will pass. It would seem to the thoughtful observer that enough had been said to stir every lover of the personal purity of his sex to fight the weed as he would fight any enemy to the welfare of "home and native land." It is a standing disgrace to our government that it is in practical partnership with both liquor and tobacco dealers, receiving from them colossal revenues each year. A nation thus supported cannot always stand. May the day speedily dawn when no unclean revenues shall enter our national treasuries.

In mercy to a suffering world, dear reader, if you use tobacco, quit it at once. Don't say you can't. Be a *man*, not a slave. If you can't quit otherwise, get medical assistance. But be sure you quit, and never begin again. At Eureka, Ill., one man, who had used tobacco twenty years, after hearing my lecture on the subject quit. Another, who had often smoked a dozen cigars in a single day, quit. Another buried his "plug" forever. I am very happy to say, that under God, I have induced men all over the land where I have lectured to quit this accursed habit, and I trust that, with the same Divine blessing upon my labors, thousands who read these lines will do likewise. If you don't quit, then the only scriptures I care to quote for your instruction are the following: "He that is filthy, let him be filthy still," and "Ephraim is joined unto his idols, let him alone."

CHAPTER V.

BAD BOOKS AND PICTURES.

Under this head I want to say a few words about obscene publications, the nude in art, and articles of immoral use. Owing to the nature of things, our pulpits and press are comparatively silent concerning these evils. And yet they are evils of great magnitude.

"No other source," says Dio Lewis, "contributes so much to sexual immorality as obscene literature. The mass of stories published in the great weeklies and the cheap novels are mischievous. When the devil determines to take charge of a young soul, he often employs a very ingenious method. He slyly hands a little novel filled with 'voluptuous forms,' 'reclining on bosoms,' 'languishing eyes,' etc. I will give you a sample passage: 'Madly, wildly bent on possessing the lovely Helene, never for an instant does his glance wander from her face and form.

With all the magnetism of fond affection firing his eyes, he stands waiting, gazing, insisting—not in vain. In an ecstacy of *abandon*, she rushes into his arms. He struggles to express in song his mad passion, and with her arms wound round about his neck, she listens, every action and look betokening the fervid, burning love that beats within her bosom, that deepens and darkens within her eyes, and lights his face like a fierce flame. Locked in each other's arms, the lovely pair, intent on each other, forget everything on earth below, and in the heavens above'— and so on for two hundred pages."

When we reflect that tons of such stuff are put on the market every month, and that multitudes of idle young ladies spend many hours a day reading the same, our only wonder is that more of them do not fall an easy prey before the subtle schemes of the libertine. Look over the publications exposed for sale at the average news depot, and what will you find? Stories of *love, crime* and *passion*. Some in yellow backs, some in red. Others in assorted colors, with highly suggestive illustrations. The prices are exceedingly low, but the moral tone of these tempting tales is infinitely lower. "Can you imagine a man born of woman, nursed and trained by maternal love, returning it all by devoting himself to the distribution of such filthy, deadly poison? None but God can measure the extent of the evil influence of these vile harpies. There are several wealthy publishers in this country whose business it is to run great steam engines and numberless machines in the preparation of this slime of the pit." It seems hard to a decent citizen that such vile assassins of purity should be allowed to remain out of jail.

"Bad books play not a small part in the corruption of youth," says Dr. Kellogg, in his widely-read pamphlet on "Social Purity." "A bad book is as bad as an evil companion. In some respects it is even worse than a living teacher of vice, since it may cling to an individual at all times. It will follow him, and poison his mind with the venom of evil. The influence of bad books in making bad boys and men is little appreciated. Few are aware how much evil seed is being sown among the young everywhere through the medium of vile books. It is not only the wretched volumes of obscenity, of which so many thousands have been seized and destroyed by Mr. Comstock, that are included under the head of bad books, and which corrupt the morals of the young, but the evil literature which is sold in nickel and dime novels, and which constitutes the principal part of the contents of such papers as the *Police Gazette*, the *Police News*, and a large proportion of the sensational story books which flood the land. You might better place a coal of fire or a live viper in your bosom, than to allow yourself to read such a book. The thoughts that are implanted in the mind in youth will often stick there through life, in spite of all efforts to dislodge them. It is an awful thing to allow the mind to be thus contaminated; and many a man would give the world, if he possessed it, to be free from the horrible incubus of a defiled imagination. Many of the papers and magazines sold at our news stands, and eagerly sought after by young men and boys, are better suited for the parlors of a house of ill-fame than for the eyes of pure-minded youth. A newsdealer who will distribute

such vile sheets ought to be dealt with as
an educator in vice and crime, an agent
of evil, and a recruiting officer of hell and
perdition."

"Sentimental literature, whether impure in its subject matter or not, has a direct tendency in the direction of impurity.
The stimulation of the emotional nature,
the instilling of sentimental ideas into
the minds of the young, has a tendency
to turn the thoughts into a channel which
leads in the direction of the formation of
vicious habits. The reading of works of
fiction is one of the most pernicious habits to which a young person can become
devoted. When the habit is once thoroughly fixed, it becomes as inveterate as
the use of liquor or opium. The novel-
devotee is as much a slave as the opium-
eater or the inebriate. The reading of
fictitious literature destroys the taste for
sober, wholesome reading, and imparts an
unhealthy stimulus to the mind, the effect
of which is in the highest degree damaging."

"I have met many cases of serious nervous disease in young ladies, in which the
real cause was nothing more nor less than

habitual novel reading. The unhealthy
state of mind engendered reacted upon
the body in such a way as to set up morbid processes, resulting in serious disease.
A fashionable malady, called by the doc-
tors *neurasthenia*, owes its origin, in not
a small proportion of cases, to the nerve-
exhausting influence of novel reading. In
this stage of haste and bustle, when all
classes of society seem to have joined in
a mad rush after diversion and excitement, what is needed is not such a literature as will excite the emotions, but such
as will calm the turbulent passions, and
afford wholesome food to promote a stable
and healthy mental growth. Many works
which are considered among the stand-
ards of literature are wholly unfit for the
perusal of young persons who wish to retain their simplicity of mind and purity of
thought. I have felt my cheeks burn
more than once when I have seen young
school girls intently poring over the vulgar poems of Chaucer, or the amorous
ditties of Burns or Byron. Still worse
than any of these are the low witticisms
of Rabelais and Boccaccio; and yet these
volumes are often found in libraries read-

ily accessible to the young. The growing influence of this kind of literature is
far more extensive than can be readily
demonstrated."

Step aboard the average passenger train
to-day and you will not much more than
have taken your seat until the news-agent
will stop before you with an armful of
books, and skillfully expose to your view
their titles, some of which are of themselves enough to make a pure and
thoughtful man ashamed to be caught
with one in his hand. Yet this is the
kind of literature thousands of men are
reading "just to pass away the time."
Stop! You have no time to "pass away."
Life is very short at best, and every moment should be well occupied. To peruse
a bad book is infinitely worse than to
"waste time." Don't do it. There are
more than 25,000 books published every
year. Select something decent, or else
don't read at all.

"You may tear your coat or break a
vase," says the Rev. T. De Witt Talmage,
"and repair it again; but the point where
the rip or fracture took place will always
be evident. It takes less than an hour to

do your heart a damage which no time can entirely repair. Look carefully over your child's library; see what book it is that he reads after he has gone to bed. Do not always take it for granted that a book is good because it is a Sunday-school book. As far as possible, know who wrote it, who illustrated it, who published it, who sold it. It seems that in the literature of the day the ten plagues of Egypt have returned, and the frogs and lice have hopped and skipped over our parlor tables. Parents are delighted to have their children read, but they should be sure as to what they read. You do not have to walk a day or two in an infected district to get the cholera or typhoid fever; and one wave of moral unhealth will fever and blast the soul forever. Perhaps, knowing not what you did, you read a bad book. Do you not remember it altogether? Yes; and perhaps you will never get over it. However strong and exalted your character, never read a bad book. By the time you get through the first chapter you will see the drift. If you find the marks of the hoofs of the devil in the picture, or in the style, or in the plot, away with it. But there is more danger, I think, from many of the family papers, published once a week, in those stories of vice and shame, full of infamous suggestions, going as far as they can without exposing themselves to the clutch of the law. I name none of them; but say that on some fashionable tables there lie 'family newspapers' that are the very vomit of the pit!'"

The following vigorous editorial, clipped from the Manhattan *Republic*, a Kansas newspaper, has the right ring. I wish every editor in America could be brought to view these matters likewise:

"We have received a proposition for an 'exchange' with the '*Police Gazette*,' the 'only illustrated sensational journal in America.' We do not need the *Gazette*, but feel disposed to give a few lines of advertising space to say that the *Police Gazette* is, in our opinion, one of the meanest, low down, vile sheets in America. It should be forbidden circulation through the mails for its obscenity. Any news dealer who keeps it for sale should be 'spotted' as a corrupter of youth; and whenever we see a man on the cars reading the *Police Gazette* we know he be-

longs to the slums. No pure-minded man
or woman ever takes it into their hands
except to put it into the fire. Richard K.
Fox, the publisher, would, in our opinion,
best serve his country behind prison bars.
'Securely wrapped' means that its abominable and obscene illustrations will be
carefully covered up so that decent friends
will not know those who revel in its nasty
pictures."

It is painful to me to see strong, intelligent men and youths reading bad books,
or feasting their eyes on filthy pictures,
for the practice is sure to affect their personal purity. Impressions will be left on
the mind which cannot fail to breed a
legion of impure thoughts, and in many
instances criminal deeds. Thousands of
elevator boys, clerks, students, traveling
men, and others, patronize the questionable literature counter to an alarming extent. Many barber shops are headquarters for vulgar papers and pictures. Here
the lustful of various ages come regularly
for this poison to mental cleanness. They
read the tinted weeklies—subtle agents of
the scarlet woman—and look with never-
waning pleasure at the pictures of half-

clothed females with which the walls are
covered. Thus the passions are aroused
and lust inflamed. What must be the
natural result? Adulteries, fornication,
lasciviousness, of course. Tobacco stores
and saloons abound with indecent pictures, fit accompaniment of their satanic
wares. It is a fearful insult to our wives,
mothers, daughters, and sisters, that so
many unprincipled business houses to-day
advertise their goods with pictures of females in semi-nude costume. Pictures
exposing the breasts and limbs of fair
women are used to advertise almost everything from beer and tobacco up to dry
goods and agricultural machinery. Theatrical managers are notoriously vulgar in
this respect. Many of the bill-boards
with which our cities are afflicted are
pasted with pictures far more suggestive
of the house of ill-fame than of a respectable entertainment. In one of our eastern
towns a certain theatrical company used
posters and lithographs representing their
female dancers in tights and low-necked
bodices. So excessively vulgar were they
that the good women of one of the

churches expressed their indignation by tacking aprons over the pictures.

It is the duty of every true man to set his influence in battle array against these enemies of decency. It is a standing disgrace to civilization that our loved ones cannot go to school or church, to market or office, without passing bill-boards and windows which expose pictures vile enough to make a savage blush.

"I suppose if we stop to think for a single moment," says Rev. Dr. Leonard, in an address before the New York Society for the Prevention of Vice, "we may all readily understand what effect an impure picture or an impure book has upon the mind of the child or youth. I remember to-night an instance in my boyhood, when I was not more than twelve years of age, and was shown a book—a vile book—by a German shoemaker. He came through the region of country where I lived, and the pictures that were in that book are now in my mind to-night as clearly as when I first looked upon them. Other pictures of beauty have faded out, but those pictures somehow have remained; and I have said to myself again and

again, I will turn that picture away
from my memory and won't think of it
again. Yet, as often as I think of that
German shoemaker, that vile book stands
out again before my mind. And so I
think it is with childhood, gentlemen; in
the early period of life a vile picture is
hung up in the chambers of the mind, and
it remains there during all future years.
It is possible for them in youth to reform
and break away from these deadly, these
dreadful, influences, but the memory, I
think, will remain. I remember years ago
having heard John B. Gough in one of
his magnificent lectures, referring to his
early life and the experiences through
which he had passed. I remember his
saying that there were sins in his early
life that he would to God he might forget;
that he had tried to banish them from his
mind, but they would not be banished.
As we who are growing older look back
into the past, we remember how difficult
it is to blot out a picture of that kind—
how difficult it is to put it away. And so
it is extremely important to protect our
children and youth against the influences
of vile pictures."

"By books and pictures the imagination is stimulated," says Rev. Dr. Buckley. "A poor woman said to her pastor in Maine: 'I had four sons. My husband was lost at sea, and I did not want any of my boys to go to sea, and three have gone, and one more will yet go.' And he looked over the house and saw a picture with all sails set, and he said: 'Madam, that is the explanation. Your first boy had nothing to look on but that view, and he went to sea. And the second looked on that picture, and thought of his brother, and went to sea. Madam, if you had sixteen children, and no other picture, they would all go to sea.' Pictures do the work." There are tens of thousands of good pictures in the world. Why not select those only to look upon which will elevate and refine the soul?

For years there has been a great craze after the nude in art, and the realistic in literature. Many art galleries abound in pictures and statuary which cannot fail to fan the fires of sensualism, unless the thoughts of the visitor are trained to the strictest purity. I believe in art. I like beautiful paintings and chisellings. And we can have all this without pandering to lust. Why should artists and sculptors persist in shocking the finer sensibilities of old and young of both sexes by crowding upon their view representations of naked human forms in attitudes of luxurious *abandon?* Public taste may demand it. But let those who have the power endeavor to reform public taste. Public taste demands many things that are unhealthful. The world abounds in lovely landscapes, fragrant flowers, beautiful birds, and varied subjects for sweetest study, to say nothing of the human form decently clothed. There is a wonderful power in art for good or evil. "In a lonely street of Florence, Michael Angelo found a fine block of marble imbedded in the mire. He dug about it, soiling his holiday attire, for, said he, 'there's an angel in it!' He felt that it was his mission to let the angel out, and he did it." Many talented artists, we fear, let demons out.

Photography is one of the marvels of the age. Its power for good can hardly be over estimated. But it also has a power for evil. Some of the photographs exhibited on our streets border very close on the vulgar, although bearing all the marks of refined art. Do you see that photographer's show-case? Yes. Do you see that young man standing before it? Yes; what of it? He is feasting his eyes on a certain photograph. It is not a photograph of a pretty babe, or a romping boy, or a noble-faced mother. Oh, no! These are too tame to stop the average young man as he hurries along the busy street. What is it then? A photograph of an idle female who thought it entertaining and nice to pose before the camera with bare arms and breasts, and, perhaps, her lower limbs clothed only in tights. Many females dress and pose as if the form were the principal thing, and the features—unfailing exponent of the soul —a secondary matter entirely. Photographs of actresses in sensualistic costumes are eagerly sought after by many men, not to mention a still worse class of pictures which the advertiser cautions the buyer to keep under lock and key. The obscene picture business is an evil of no small magnitude. Up to March 1, 1892, Mr. Anthony Comstock reports his

confiscation of over five thousand negative plates for making obscene pictures,
and over eight hundred thousand pictures and photos.   This is just one item
in the work of one society during a period
of only twenty years.   How many millions of such bad pictures are still extant
nobody knows.   Dear reader, if you have
an obscene picture in your possession,
destroy it at once.   Don't give it away,
for it might corrupt a hundred hearts.
Destroy it.   Your personal purity will
certainly be contaminated if you form the
habit of feasting your eyes upon lewd
illustrations.   Likewise if you have a bad
book in your possession, destroy it.   Never
put it into another's hands.   It might lead
to the ruin of many bodies and the damnation of many souls.   Oh, the evil influence of bad books and pictures!

" Good men have ever lamented the pernicious influence of a depraved and perverted literature," says the Prison Association of New York, in one of its reports.
" But such literature has never been so
systematically and widely diffused as at
the present time.   This is owing to two
causes, its cheapness, and the facility of

conveyance by steamboat and rail car. A very large proportion of the works thus put in circulation are of the worst character, tending to corrupt the principles, to inflame the passions, to excite impure desire, and to spread a blight over all the powers of the soul. Brothels are recruited from this more than any other one source. Those who search the trunks of convicted criminals are almost sure to find in them one or more of these works; and few prisoners who can read at all fail to enumerate among the causes which led them into crime the unhealthy stimulus of this depraved and pernicious literature."

"Many years ago, in another land," says Rev. Dr. John Hall, "I was called from my bed about two or three o'clock of a winter morning and requested to go some distance to see a man that believed himself to be dying. He was a perfect stranger to me, but of course it was my duty as minister of the gospel to respond promptly to the call, and I went. He was in a dying condition. His body was weak and poor, exhausted, but his mind was clear and distinct. Hardly ever have I

heard from any human creature a more
distinct and pronounced confession of sin
and acknowledgment of guiltiness before
God than I heard from that man. I
prayed with him again and again. At
his request, I kneeled down at his bedside and prayed with him. The poor man
tried to get out of bed and go on his
knees to show how earnest he was. After
a time, he spoke of his career, and he made
this statement, giving me directions to go
to a particular trunk in his room, and
gave the key to me. He said, 'In the
trunk you will see there is a large parcel
of books. Those are bad books, corrupt
books; I would be ashamed to show them
to anybody that knew mé; they have been
destructive to me in body, and I believe,
in soul, and I want you to take those
books away and burn them, that they may
never go into other hands.' I took the
books and locked them up in my own study
until I could have a whole day in the
study, and I did burn the books, and I can
tell you it is a very slow process burning
books; but I had some satisfaction in feeling that that which according to that
man's testimony had ruined him would

never be the ruin of any other human creature."

But oh, the value and joy of a pure book! What an influence it exerts over our hearts for good. "Books are the best things, well used," says Emerson, "abused, among the worst." "A good book," says Milton, "is the precious life-blood of a master spirit, embalmed and treasured up on purpose to a life beyond." "A wise man," says Langford, "will select his books, for he would not wish to class them all under the sacred name of friends. Some can be accepted only as acquaintances. The best books of all kinds are taken to the heart and cherished as his most precious possessions."

Concerning articles of immoral use, I have little to say. A moment's thought should be sufficient to enlist the sympathies of every pure soul against this evil. Our newspapers frequently contain advertisements of pills and medicines for the use of those anxious to commit the terrible sin of abortion. Tons of such commodities are sold every year. Unprincipled manufacturers in several parts of our country are constantly plying a subtle trade in various articles for the prevention of conception. Mr. Comstock has seized nearly one hundred thousand such articles, of rubber, etc., and these astonishing figures probably do not represent one-tenth of the magnitude of this evil. The crime of abortion, together with the desire to prevent pregnancy, is on the increase, and hence the demand for these unhallowed goods. Many of these devices used in the prevention of conception are both filthy and injurious. Decent men should scorn the thought, much more the use, of these abominable contrivances. Decent newspapers should respect the purity of their constituency too highly to advertise such lust-breeding wares. Decent druggists and other dealers should take pride enough in cleanliness to rid their secret shelves and drawers of every illegitimate article of merchandise. The health and personal purity of the race is of far more consequence to a respectable man than the few ducats he might be able to extract from the pockets of sensualists in the sale of questionable goods of whatever nature.

CHAPTER VI.

GAMBLING; OR, THE ART OF GETTING SOMETHING FOR NOTHING.

The sin of gambling is multiplying itself to-day with fearful rapidity. Gambling is the art of getting something for nothing. It is a sin which is corrupting thousands of men from nearly every walk of life. And yet comparatively little literature can be found on the subject. The public conscience is not yet awakened to the enormity of the evil. Hence many men are blindly led into the practice, and find themselves under the fascinating power of the habit before realizing its exceeding sinfulness. No man can long retain his personal purity who gives himself over to this subtle agent of hell.

"I have no patience with men who gamble," says Rev. Dr. McArthur, of New York, in a recent address. "There is a perfect mania in our country just now

for gambling. I have been through many
parts of New England during the past
few months, and I am told by clergymen
and others in many manufacturing towns
that there is such a mania for gambling
as has not been known in twenty years.
Pools are formed, small contributions are
received, and a large number of young
men—the boys who are working in the
mills and in the factories—are engaged in
this dangerous undertaking. A boy who
will gamble will steal. Gambling is a
species of theft. A boy who wants something for nothing is a dishonest boy. A
man who says 'the world owes me a living
and I propose to have it,' is a worthless
and dishonest man. The world does not
owe him a living. The world owes a man
what he will earn, nothing more, nothing
less, and every man that engages in gambling is striving with all his might to get
something for nothing.''

I will quote a few paragraphs from Mr.
Anthony Comstock's report for 1890 to
the New York Society for the Prevention
of Vice. These paragraphs touch upon
several different phases of the gambling

evil, and are almost enough to make one's blood run cold:—

"We are not permitted to forget the curse of gambling and lotteries, for an incessant string of complaints reaches our office in the *Times* building, either by mail or by persons calling. Some of these complaints would almost melt a heart of stone. They demand attention in many cases because they are the pathetic wail of starving women and helpless children, beggared because husbands, fathers and sons are ground to poverty and crime between the stones of the gamblers' remorseless mill.

"One morning, in January last, a publisher called, relating that at a certain place in this city, his brother, twenty years of age, had recently lost $14,000 at gambling, a part of which did not belong to him.

"Another day, last summer, a mother with a nursing babe in her arms called to complain against 'Big Mike' Murray's den in East Fourteenth Street, because her husband was upon the verge of suicide, having lost all their savings for years, amounting to about $3,000. This lady has had to give up home and pawn almost everything she had, in order to support herself and her babe, being forced to move from a comfortable home into squalid quarters in the rear of a tenement house.

"A merchant in Duane Street called one afternoon to complain of two places in Park Row, near the bridge, where one of his clerks had been led astray. This clerk had embezzled funds from his employer, beggared his wife and three little children, and was then upon the verge of suicide. This merchant had scarcely left the office before in walked a young lawyer, a son of a late member of the Assembly of our State, he also having a wife and three children, and almost the first words he uttered were: 'If you do not close up a certain gambling place (naming it), I shall take my life. I cannot stand it to see my wife and children suffer. I know I am a fool to do it, but if I have a dollar I cannot go by that place.' We raided two of these places, and arrested and convicted thirteen gamblers found in them.

"In September last, a young son of a millionaire, who had squandered his inheritance in riotous living, and also spent funds belonging to others at the gaming table, was about to be married to a beautiful young lady. The wedding day came. The guests and minister had assembled to celebrate the marriage, when all at once the groom was missing! Shortly afterward, his dead body was found with a most heart-rending and pitiful letter, written the day before, left to his beloved, from which we quote as follows: 'To-morrow is the time set for our wedding. You are happy at its near approach, while I am unhappy, dejected, and on the brink of the grave. Broken down in spirits and in health, and ruined financially, as my appearance indicates, I hasten to end my misery. I will no longer torture your feelings by keeping you in suspense: So strong was my propensity for gambling that I was utterly powerless to stop it while a dollar remained. I went on till all I could touch of my own property and the funds entrusted to me by my deceased friend were buried in the accursed vortex which had already swallowed up so much from me.'

"The suicide of the late cashier of the New York Postoffice is fresh in the

minds of all. After his death, the fact
was discovered that he had been a victim
of the gambling mania, and had sent bootblacks and others to carry his money over
from the postoffice to neighboring pool-
rooms, there to bet upon horse races with
the book-making sharps.

"Only a few days ago, this community
was shocked by the account of the downfall and suicide of a prominent society
man in Albany. He resided in a beautiful home with his five motherless little
children. He was in a position of high
trust and responsibility, and enjoyed the
confidence of his employers. After em-
bezzling over $100,000, he was discovered,
and he took his own life, leaving his little
ones so destitute that neighbors were
obliged to contribute for the bare necessities of life. The newspapers print the
horrors of these gambling crimes in one
column, and advertise the pool and horse-
race gamblers in another. Murders and
suicides occur frequently as the direct
harvest of this kind of seed-sowing. Men
read them and pass them by with scarcely
a thought. Not so in our office. We are
brought face to face with the sorrow,

misery and suffering of the gamblers'
victims. Crimes run riot in the community because of the gambling mania.
One of our daily papers, in March, contained an editorial giving an account of
the sentence to state's prison of the city
treasurer of Rochester for embezzlement;
of the defalcation of the state treasurer
of Maryland, the state treasurer of Kentucky, and the flight from justice of the
state treasurer of Louisiana, because of
an alleged defalcation of over half a million of dollars. At the same time, it
spoke of the city treasurer of Chattanooga,
Tenn., for making away with the funds
of that city also.

"A few weeks ago, a man in New York
City committed suicide after securing
$250 of his wife's savings from the Four-
teenth Street Savings Bank and losing it
at policy.   With his dead body was found
a note to his wife, saying: 'The policy-
shops in Fourth Street and Sixth Street
have been my ruin.'

"Friends, you must regard us as something less than human if you expect us to
be brought in contact with such scenes,
the results of the curse of gambling, and

not move with all our hearts to the
defense of these innocent victims of this
shameless and heartless fraternity. But
this is not all. We cannot stop here.
We have a scrap-book in our office that
contains a partial record of the results of
gambling, as furnished by the daily press.
This record shows only a tithe of the real
results, but these facts are appalling facts.
The following is a synopsis from this record of

CRIMES ARISING FROM GAMBLING DURING 1890:

"One hundred and twenty-eight persons
were either shot or stabbed over gambling
games. Four were stabbed and five shot
at poker. Twelve stabbed and twenty-
four shot over the game of craps, a game
of dice much played by bootblacks and
newsboys, upon the sidewalk, and by fast
young men and negroes. Twenty-eight
were stabbed, and fifty-five were shot
over the gaming-table, or as the direct result thereof. Besides these, six attempted
suicide, twenty-four committed suicide,
and sixty persons were murdered in cold
blood, while two were driven insane.
Sixty-eight youth and persons have been

ruined by pool-gambling and betting upon horse-racing. Among the crimes committed to get money to gamble with are two burglaries, eighteen forgeries, and eighty-five embezzlements, while thirty-two persons holding positions of trust in banks and other places of mercantile life absconded. The enormous sum of $2,898,-372 is shown by this same record as the proceeds of these embezzlements and defalcations. To these crimes must be added the long list of thefts, robberies, embezzlements, larcenies and defalcations, which are never known except to immediate friends or persons especially interested. But what of broken-hearted fathers, mothers, husbands, wives and children, who are ruthlessly hurled from happy homes, comfortable circumstances, and social positions through these crimes and criminals? Is there no pity for these helpless women and children? Shall no one strike a blow in their defense? We have been striking blow after blow by the arrest of professional gamblers and their 'touts,' the seizing of their paraphernalia, and the closing of their dens of glittering temptations. We plead these facts as the strongest arguments why our efforts to enforce the laws should be sustained.

"During the past year, we have raided fifty-two gambling places, and seized as follows: 7 faro, 8 roulette, 4 rouge et noir, 4 hazard layouts, and tables, one sweat board, 16,900 chips, 203,783 lottery tickets, 64,356 lottery circulars, 245,347 pool tickets, 14,861 lottery policies, besides a quantity of other gambling paraphernalia!"

The following item, just clipped from a daily paper, is one among hundreds of similar nature constantly appearing:—

CALDWELL, Kas., May 1. — Charles Smith, a prominent young man of this place, was shot and killed this afternoon over a game of cards by Bert Williams, a bar-tender. Williams was arrested by the sheriff, who thus far has been able to keep himself and his prisoner in hiding for fear of lynching. A mob has been formed and is making every endeavor to find the murderer. Williams is a recent arrival from Dayton, Ohio.

The Lottery business has long been an evil of great magnitude in this country. It is a dangerous form of gambling, and annually leads thousands astray. Many church members, as well as "thugs," seem to think there is no moral wrong in purchasing a few lottery tickets from time to time. But hear the decision of the Supreme Court of the United States as handed down by Chief Justice Waite: "That lotteries are demoralizing in their effects, no matter how carefully regulated, cannot, in the opinion of this Court, be doubted. They are a species of gambling, and wrong in their influences. They disturb the checks and balances of a well-ordered community." And Judge Caton, of whom some one has said, "His opinion delivered from both the Supreme Court of his State and from that of the nation will ever be regarded as of highest authority," said in the well-known case of Smith and Lane *vs.* the State of Tennessee: "Lotteries are gambling and odious gambling."

The celebrated Louisiana State Lottery has been a bitter curse to our country from its very beginning. It has wheedled millions upon millions of dollars out of the pockets of the masses. I am glad that recent legislative enactments practically doom the lottery business in the United

States. But Mexico is not far away, and already her lotteries are raking in thousands from the gullible in the States. It was P. T. Barnum, the great showman, I believe, who said "the American people love to be humbugged." The lottery is a dangerous species of humbug. The whole tendency is evil, and no man who respects true industry, honesty, and sobriety, should ever countenance the pest for a moment.

By way of illustration, I will quote an anecdote from the Rev. Dr. Arvine's "Cyclopædia." It is one among thousands of similar ones, I suppose, which, if collected and printed, would make a startling book. But one is enough to arrest the attention of those who are not too far gone :—

"In 1833, an adventurer in lotteries committed suicide in the city of Boston by drowning himself. The fate of this unfortunate man contains one of those impressive moral lessons which address us with a power which no uninspired lips can do. He was in the employment of one of the most respectable houses in the city, highly esteemed and respected by the members of it, and in the receipt of a liberal salary. About a year before, he had the misfortune to draw a prize in the lottery, and from that moment his fate was sealed. The regular earnings of honest industry were not enough for him —visions of splendid prizes were continually floating before his eyes, and he plunged at once into the excitement of lotteries. He soon became deeply involved, and his access to the funds of the firm held out to him a temptation which he could not resist. He appropriated to himself considerable sums from time to time, continually deluded by the hope that a turn of the wheel would give him the means of replacing them. But that turn never came; fortune gave him but one smile, and that was a fatal one. He saw that detection would soon come, and that the punishment and the shame of a felon would succeed the consideration and respect he had always enjoyed, and he had not courage to wait the moment of disclosure. He sought refuge in death, thus adding to his other sins the horrible act of self-murder! He left a memorandum which contained an account of the circumstances that made life intolerable to him."

Dealing in futures under the rules and regulations of modern "Boards of Trade" has come to be another dangerous pitfall to men. Whatever may be said in the defense of these institutions, they are, nevertheless, closely akin to regularly ordained gambling dens and lotteries. In the great Chicago Board of Trade, millions of bushels of fictitious grain are bought and sold on margins, and sometimes the saddest results follow these wild speculations. I have more than once sat and watched the "bulls" and "bears" in the wheat pit of this great institution; and I cannot refrain from saying that it is almost enough to make angels weep sometimes to witness what consummate fools many men make of themselves in order to pile up a little gold. Legitimate trading in actual products is all right. But the tendency of dealing in futures is all wrong.

From the Rev. Dr. Arvine's work, to which reference has already been made, I extract the following paragraphs, illustrating, first, the fact that gambling is largely sustained by deception and fraud; second, that it is a sin which destroys natural sensibility—blunts every noble conception as to the eternal fitness of things; third, that it often leads to the direst temporal and spiritual consequences:—

"Cheats are used in horse-racing as in other species of gambling. There was a man in Kentucky noted for making match races; and a club of men went to the expense of procuring a fast horse in order to beat one he boasted much of. The jockey closed the agreement for the race with a bet of about $2,000; and the club was very certain of beating the jockey. When the day arrived for the race, and the horses started, the club's horse went ahead of the jockey's immediately, and took the inside track. At the first turn, he fell to his knees, and while recovering himself the slow horse got ahead of him. After running some distance, the fast horse fell again, and the slow horse won the race. The fast horse became lame from his fall. His owners were much chagrined at their misfortune, and on the next morning went to the jockey's lodgings in order to close another race

with him. The landlord informed them
that he had left the night before, soon
after the race was over. His sudden departure, after a successful race, excited
suspicions of foul play. They then examined the track, and found that the
jockey had dug a number of small holes
on the inside of the same, placing gourds
in them, and spreading a little loose dirt
over them; and when the fast horse ran
close to the fence he would tread on
these gourds, sinking and stumbling, and
thus giving the slow one the advantage.
When this discovery was made, they
decided on having another race at all
events, and so chased the jockey nearly a
hundred miles, but did not succeed in
overtaking him.

"Well did Dr. Nott say 'the finished
gambler has no heart—he would play at
his brother's funeral—he would gamble
upon his mother's coffin!' Horace Wal-
pole mentions an anecdote of a man having in his time dropped down at the door
of White's club house, into which he was
carried. The members of the club immediately made bets as to whether he was
dead or not; and upon its being proposed

to bleed him, the wagerers for his death interposed, alleging that it would affect the fairness of the bet!

"The desperate depravity to which gambling reduces its votaries is strikingly illustrated in the case of three gamblers here related. They determined on a game which was doubtless meant to show their contempt of all things sacred in this world and the next. Accordingly, they enter at night the charnel house and take from thence a corpse that very day placed in the vault. They bear the deceased into the cathedral, pass within the chancel, light up one of the candles before the altar, seat the grim corpse by the *communion table*, and, gathering around the table themselves, proceed to engage in a game of cards! Shameless, sacrilegious doings that none but gamblers could think of without shuddering!! This incident is said by Rev. Wm. B. Tappan, of Boston, to rest on good authority, and he has accordingly made it the occasion of a short poem on gambling.

"I was well acquainted," says Mr. Green, the reformed gambler, "with the circumstance of a young man starting to

go to the hot springs of Arkansas. He
was a man who had acquired by honesty and industry about $900. He had
been in bad health for some time, and
concluded to visit the springs to recruit.
On his arrival at the mouth of White
River, he was detained for a boat, and
while there was induced to play cards. I
am unable to say at this time what the
game was that he played, but he won
some forty or fifty dollars and the game
broke up. After the game was broken up,
one of the gamblers pulled out a button
and bantered the young man to win it at
'faro.' He pulled out a quarter and bet it
against the button, and the banker won.
He tried again and again until he lost
some three or four dollars to win that
button, and then went to bed. The
banker had now several persons betting
small bets on the game, and had won some
eight or ten dollars, and there was quite a
noise and bustle going on. The young
man, who had quit and gone to bed, got
up and felt a strong propensity to win all.
He began betting on the game again, and
in a short time lost the whole of his $900
trying to win a button! For that was all

he could have won, as the man had at
first no money except what he had won
from the young man. The young man
was obliged to make his way home without his health being benefited and without his money.

"A colored fireman on board a steamboat running from St. Louis to New
Orleans, having lost all his money at
poker with his companions, staked his
clothing, and being still unfortunate,
pledged his own freedom for a small
amount. Losing this, the bets were
doubled, and he finally, at one desperate
hazard, ventured his own value as a slave,
and laid down his free papers to represent
the stake. He lost, suffered his certifi-
cates to be destroyed, and was actually
sold by the winner to a slave dealer, who
hesitated not to take him at a small discount upon his asserted value!"

Thousands of similar illustrations might
be collected. But these will suffice to
show to what fatal extremes this terrible
sin can lead its votaries. There is a fearful fascination about this evil, and no
man should risk himself by even so much
as learning the tricks of gamblers merely

for pastime. And let me cry out right here with all my strength against the all-too-common practice of card-playing in the home for amusement. Many professing Christians argue that it is safer to teach their boys to play cards at home, for then they will not care to visit gaming places to practice this art mysterious. What inexcusable foolishness! What father would teach his boy to swear at home, thus hoping to forestall his swearing abroad? What mother would teach her son to drink at home and assist him in the cultivation of a healthy appetite for liquor, thus hoping to prevent his getting drunk abroad? But this would be just as wise as to teach the boy cards. It stands to reason that the average lad who can play well at home will sooner or later want to display his ability abroad. And he will do it too. He may not bet at first. But look out! There is danger ahead. One taste of victory in gambling and he is gone. It is a startling fact that there are very few reformed gamblers. "There is nothing," says Steele, "that wears out a fine face like the vigils of the card-table

and those cutting passions which naturally attend them."

Oh, parents, I implore you, set your
faces like flint against cards. I speak of
this particular game because it is by far
the most common and potent for evil.
Perhaps nine-tenths of all the gambling
in Satan's dens is conducted with cards.
So true is this that the very words
"poker" and "euchre" seem almost syn-
onymous with *hell*. I would not exclude
from this comparison the modern fashionable game of "progressive euchre," often
engaged in by prominent and popular
church members. The Rev. Sam Jones,
though harsh, was not far wrong when
he styled this new diversion "progressive
damnation." No respectable man should
play cards, much less gentlemen and
ladies who claim to be followers of the
meek and lowly Nazarene.

"But do you condemn amusements altogether?" inquires a friend.

By no means. Amusements are necessary. In this roaring, boiling, seething
nineteenth century life, they are indis-
pensable to the man who would not break
down long before his time. But there are

many good and wholesome amusements which remove the imagined necessity of resorting to cards. "Authors," "logamachy," etc., are not only amusing, but instructive. "croquet," "lawn tennis," etc., are both amusing and healthful.

"But are not "authors" *cards*? and is it not just as bad to play this game as 'euchre' or 'poker' ?"

No. Gamblers never play "authors." Such games are too tame and refined for them. The Apostle Paul, writing to the Thessalonians, says, "Abstain from all appearance of evil" (1 Thess. 5: 22). The cards used by gamblers would certainly fall under the condemnation of this text, for with their black and red spots and grotesque figures they seem a fitting picture of the bottomless pit.

Father, do you value your boys' present and eternal welfare at all? If so, never let a card come into your house. It would be just as sensible for you to bring home a nest of young vipers, and, putting them in your wife's work-basket, say, "Boys, go in mamma's room and play now," as to bring home a "deck" of cards, and, placing them upon the center table of the sitting room, say, "Boys, stay in here and play now." They would soon learn the fatal game, and nine chances to one their precious souls would be blighted forever. It would be infinitely better in the long run to bury your boys from the sting of the adder's bite, than to corrupt their souls beyond the probability of redemption by teaching them the devil's favorite game.

Boys should never be allowed to play marbles for "keeps." This is undoubtedly with thousands a first step toward gambling. The expression "I'll bet you so-and-so" should never be used by those who value a pure and wholesome conversation. The betting of cigars or small amounts of money on trifling results, often lead into the habit of gambling. No man should bet on anything. The custom of betting on elections is one to be deplored by all good citizens. There is nothing manly about it, but on the other hand much that borders on the heathenish.

Have you ever been guilty of gambling, dear reader? Have you ever let yourself down beneath the true dignity of a noble manhood by betting, gaming for money, risking at lottery, or anything of this nature? If so, I entreat you, *stop*, and *stop now*.

> "Unless above himself he can
> Erect himself, how poor a thing is man."

Rise above your baser desires. Trample under foot every inclination to get something for nothing. Be a man, and an honest one at that. Pope says,

> "An honest man's the noblest work of God."

And another,

> "Man is his own star; and that soul that can
> Be honest is the only perfect man."

CHAPTER VII.

THE SOCIAL EVIL; OR, ADULTERY, FORNICATION
AND KINDRED CRIMES.

If there is any subject under heaven
needing plain and pointed discussion to-
day, it is the one now before us. And
yet it is one sadly neglected by pulpit and
press, owing, perhaps, to its peculiar
delicateness on the one hand, and to a
manufactured modesty on the other.

"It is a dreadful comment on the so-
called modesty of the Christian world,"
says Joseph Waddell Clokey, "that its magazines, newspapers and pulpits have been
almost wholly silent on the so-called social vices. Hush! hush! the refined have
cried at every public reference to them,
till licentiousness has well-nigh under-
mined our social fabric. Its prevalence is
truly appalling. The better classes have
been ignorant of it, because it is a malady
that moves in silence and preys on its

victims in the night-time and in concealment. It has no plain advertisements in
the newspapers; pastes up no flaming
posters; glows with no electric lights; is
surrounded by no bands of music. It is
this secrecy that leaves so many parents
and reformers in ignorance, and, when the
thin veil is lifted, makes them incredulous
of what is revealed."

Various books touching more or less on
the subject have been written, chiefly by
medical practitioners, many of whom, it is
believed, care more about the business
phase of the question than the moral.
Thus the evil is growing, and with fearful rapidity. We are, as a nation, becoming shamefully unchaste. Sins that
shocked our forefathers and called forth
the severest condemnation are now
winked at in average social circles. Adulteries, fornications, and kindred crimes,
are more common in America to-day than
ever before.

"This is one of the most important subjects that could engage the mind of man,"
says Prof. H. I. Bryant, in a lecture on
"Social Purity," "and yet it is one of the
most sadly neglected. While it has been

dealt with in a general way by the press and from the pulpit for centuries, this manner has not been successful in effecting the end desired. What means this lamentation over the decay of morals and virtue? Bishops and sages tell us they are waning. Is it true? If ever there was a time in the history of any country when the moral tide was lower, may God pity the generation of that time. There are more libertines among men than ever before. They work more successful schemes on young and innocent girls than in any other age of the world—more cunning and artful.

"Seducing women is now a studied art among libertines; and it is pursued by more students than is any branch of science or literature. It has more graduates than any department of all our institutions of learning, and they are more successful in their chosen profession. Women are not always guiltless. Almost every city has its bawdy houses, and many of them hundreds. They have their thousands of inmates, many of whom are girls between eight and twelve years old. Death takes pity on them and re-

lieves them from a life of misery and
shame ere their allotted days are numbered.
They too are engaged in the work of
capturing others. They flaunt themselves
before you in a most enticing manner.
They draw many youths into their dens
of vice, and gild their souls with sin.
Nor is this public life of shame the fullest
extent of this crime. It is to be found in
all classes of society. Among men it is
the general rule, to which the virtuous are
exceptions; among women it is wonder-
fully common. I would not unveil the
secrets of their hearts. I would to God
that the world did not know so much of
their sins as it does. But their stories
have oft been told. Nature does not
always keep their secrets, and men seldom
do.

"The late Bishop Burrows, of London,
England, exposes this sin, with others, in
the wealthy church of which he was pastor. He said that from a long time past
he had known of this corruption and
crime within his fold, but had not, until
now, dared to speak of it only in generali-
ties, but that he could endure it no longer.
He then proceeded to denounce them in a

bold and fearless manner, and a more cutting denunciation I have never read. He told them that he had sat in the house with whores and whoremongers, not daring to raise his voice against them. And he said, 'there are ladies whose faces I see here to-night with whom no decent tradesman's wife or daughter would associate.

"The time has come when we must deal with this subject specifically. We can smother the truth no longer; cold-blooded facts stare us in the face. Something must be done to check this tide of sin that sweeps us down toward hell, or we shall be entombed in its awful gulf. This sad state of affairs exists to-day in more churches than are to be found in the world's metropolis. The crime of adultery is common, and is said to be on the increase."

One honorable physician declares that ninety males out of a hundred cohabit with women before marriage. I trust that this estimate is too high, and yet some excellent authorities believe the percentage to be even higher. An old physician of unimpeached character is reported by

Mr. Clokey to have said: "When I was a young man, not one young woman in twenty was solicited for her ruin; now I sometimes think that not one in twenty escapes solicitation."

In 1890, I was secretary of the Ministerial Educational Society, of Kansas. We assisted several young men in Garfield University, Wichita, that year. To our chagrin one of the most promising of the number was found guilty of visiting bad women, and expelled from the institution. When first approached on the subject he strenuously denied his guilt, but afterward made full confession. Thus this subtle sin made this young man both a liar and a fornicator, and brought shame to his instructors, his classmates, his mother, and his sacred profession.

Chancellor Everest informed me that there were estimated to be 500 prostitutes in Wichita at that time—a city of less than 40,000 inhabitants.

"If my hack could only talk, Pete," said a driver to a friend of mine, "it would tell some startling tales, but it can't, and I dare not." This driver asserted that some of the "best" people of the city, married and unmarried, were patrons of his hack in still hours of the night, and this in a locality noted for its culture.

Startling as these disclosures may be, is it not high time that somebody should cry out against such crimes? They cannot be cured by keeping silent. Oh, no! Silence is the patron saint of lust. Let the secrets of modern libertinism, in high as well as low estate, be revealed, and this form of sin would receive a most salutary check. This is a time noted for its domestic infelicities and divorces. I believe that lust and sexual unfaithfulness are the chief causes for this deplorable state of things. It is a common occurrence nowadays for the papers to publish all the details that decency will allow concerning the unfaithfulness of a husband or the waywardness of a wife. Certainly the social evil has come to be one of appalling magnitude.

"It is not considered much of a disgrace for man to commit fornication," says Prof. Bryant in his plain, pungent style. "Do you ask why? Because such is the ethics of society. So common is this crime

among men that the youth of to-day
thinks that he cannot be a man until he
has been guilty of it. And when he has
committed the act he cannot rest until he
has gone to all his friends and told it.
He'll tell it by way of 'putting the boys
on.' So honorable, so dignified, to him, is
this boasted sinning that he will often lie
like a thief about it. He'll say he did,
when he didn't. Thus has many an innocent girl been stigmatized—branded
unto the end of life by a lie told to make
the youth of the nineteenth century a
man. They congregate on the street
corners to tell their experiences, and full
grown men will do the same. What is it
that old grey-haired deacon was telling
the other day? Oh, it was just a little
piece of his experience when he was a
boy—before he got religion you know.
Got religion! If *he* should become a
Christian all at once it would be such a
sudden shock to his nervous system that
he would collapse. He ought to be
ashamed of himself. The man who will
sit around and tell the boys of his mean
tricks before he was 'converted,' has
never been converted. He would do the

very same thing again if he had a chance. He would step over the line at the drop of the hat, and he would drop the hat himself at that. I have no patience with such fellows. I think more of a genuine dude than I do of such a fellow. These are the fellows that sit around on dry-goods boxes windy days watching for the wind to blow the passing lady's dress to get to see her stockings, and then signficantly tell how many stripes they have. Some of these fellows are eternally on the rack hunting 'soft snaps,' and when he has found one the next thing is to hunt the boys up and 'give them a pointer.' He tells them how he 'had to rustle.' Yes, poor girl. How she struggled against her own passions and his entreaties. Noble effort she made, but she was defeated, and now he is telling how he accomplished it, and what a 'honey' she is. Were you to hear him describe her bust, limbs, and all her voluptuous beauty, you would think he was describing the goddess Venus de Medici. If there is one in that crowd who has nothing to boast of, Oh, how mean he feels. He wants to go off and ' kick himself' when he thinks what might have been. He feels disgraced and must do something to redeem himself. It won't do, he is away behind the times. If you want to insult a youth of to-day, and have tried every other means and failed, after you have exhausted your vocabulary of mean epithets without effecting your purpose, just call him a *nice, virtuous boy*, and you will stir his ire from the depths of his soul. He may stand it to be called dishonest, a liar and a thief, but he can't have the dignity of his manhood insulted in that way."

Let us glance at some of the causes of this evil:

"The corruption of morals," says one writer, "arises in part from the despotism of governments, from disproportion in rank, and from extreme inequality in fortunes. Deprived of political rights by the sovereignty of an individual, the subjects make amends by precipitating themselves into pleasures, and despots favor sensuality in order to reign more easily over an enervated people. We shall always notice a great demoralization in the countries where men of power possess all, while the people attached to the cultivation of the soil have nothing of their own. The slave becomes perverted, the master dissolute. The slave has the shameful glory of corrupting his master, and the latter has in his hand the power to satisfy his libidinous caprices and the fortune to pursue his pleasures."

"It is easy to find other causes for libertinism, prostitution and the viler crimes of a kindred nature," says another. "First, the law of hereditary transmission, which almost invariably decrees a vicious child to a licentious father. This fact all history proves. Messalina was the daughter of Lepida, a debauched prostitute. Julia, the daughter of Augustus, was as bad as her father, and gave birth to a child of equally strong propensities. The social causes that conduce to these crimes are many and various. Men encourage, rather than restrain their worst passions, and women, in ignorance and vanity, offer no opposition to the libertine's advances. The idleness of most young girls in what is called our 'first society' is a fruitful mother of mischief. Their minds are not fed by nourishing food, and they seek abnormal gratification. They become morbid, restless and melancholy, and are soon ready to admit suggestions of evil. The case of the working-girl who loses her virtue is still more sad. Hunger and unkindness assail her. Her bloom fades. Her future is a black distance into which she dare not look. Temptation comes to her whose weakness should be a protection against the basest libertine that breathes. Warmth and comfort and love are offered. Her thoughts dwell on this subject incessantly. Virtue becomes at last an idle name to her, not the symbolic word whose translation is a pure life. She falls, and her fatal course can never be retraced. In houses of prostitution exceptional cases are often found—girls who have been drugged and violated, others who live degraded lives for the sake of the money it enables them to give to helpless relatives, and a still smaller number possessing constitutions so libidinous that they voluntarily choose the life which best gratifies their ungovernable passions."

The fast living of these modern times is undoubtedly a most fruitful cause of sexual incontinency in all its phases. Highly seasoned foods, exciting stimulants, and late hours are working incalculable mischief every day. "Fashionable life," says Dr. Kellogg, "with its frivolities and dissipations, is a foe to virtue. The whole tendency of modern fashionable life is in the highest degree calculated to stimulate the development of the emotional nature, which leads directly to the exaggeration of the propensities. The cultivation of the æsthetic at the expense of the practical, and the devotion to the thousand and one nothings which make up the sum total of a fashionable woman's life, are by no means conducive to the growth of purity and the repression of the animal instincts. With an untrained mind, that is, one which has not cultivated self-control and the habit of making a careful analysis of the feelings, one emotion is often converted into another seemingly wholly unlike and incompatible with the first. (Perhaps this philosophy may account for the lapses from virtue occasionally reported among religious enthusiasts.— AUTHOR.) The cultivation of the emotional nature at the expense of the reasoning faculties is on this account a most serious error.

Theatre-going, novel-reading, dancing, attendance at fashionable parties, flirtation, and a variety of other practices exceedingly common in the life of the average young lady, are the means by which the moral sense becomes depraved and the character so unbalanced as to break down the barriers to impurity, and to open the way for the encroachments of the tempter."

Concerning the modern dance alone, a volume might be written. This amusement is a deadly foe to purity, and I am glad that the pious and pure of all faiths condemn it. "All savage nations dance," says Rev. J. Cameron. "The heathen Cicero said, 'no one dances unless he is either drunk or mad.' Among the ancient Romans it was considered beneath the dignity of persons of rank and character to dance. Even the Mohammedan religion forbids dancing, and shall Christians, who claim a better religion, and a higher standard of morality, become its patrons?" Arch-Bishop Spaulding, of New York, states that the confessional of his church has revealed the fact that nineteen-twentieths of the women who fall take their first downward step in dancing parties. Mrs. Gen. W. T. Sherman, after reading "The Dance of Death," a startling attack on this modern sin, addressed its author as follows: "Women of virtue or self-respect will now blush to have the dance named to them. An amusement which leads, in any case, to such results as you have pointed out should be forever discountenanced." "The tendency of dancing," says the Rev. N. S. Haynes, a Chicago pastor, "is toward frivolity, worldliness, lust, lewdness, and hell." "I have noticed," says Evangelist Barrow, of Nebraska, "that people lose interest in Christianity when they become interested in dancing. Take from dancing all that belongs to Satan's kingdom—the tendency to lust and libertinism—and there is nothing left to make a dance of; eliminate its patent, glaring, transparent tendency toward an unholy and unlawful association of the sexes, and there will be an end of dancing."

But enough. Men who respect female virtue and manly purity will not dance. Christians who lament the alarming magnitude of the social evil should unite in

opposing the dance, for in so doing they
will remove one of the most potent causes
of adultery, fornication, and sexual looseness in general.

"The unlimited freedom allowed the
young during real or pretended courtship," says one, "is certainly not conducive to improvement in the direction of
social morality. The fashion prevalent in
some communities by which young people who are contemplating marriage may
sit up until the small hours of the morning, with curtains closely drawn and
lights turned low or extinguished, is in no
particular less inconsistent than the practice of 'bundling' which once prevailed
among the early Dutch settlers of New
York, and is still not unknown in some of
the remote rural districts of Pennsylvania. A mother who allows such a
practice under her roof must be considered accessory to the consequences.
Fathers and mothers who wish to preserve the purity of their sons and daughters should make a vigorous protest
against the growing looseness of manners
and unrestrained freedom of social intercourse among the sexes, whether carried

on under the guise of courtship, or without the cover of this flimsy excuse. There was a time in the history of the world when a young man who had committed a gross crime against virtue was considered unfit to live, and was taken without the city and pelted to death with stones. At the present time, a young man who is known to be a rake is made welcome to the most aristocratic circles of society, and often receives as much or even greater attention from fashionable young women, and older women too, than those whose lives are spotless."

Here is undoubtedly one of the most prolific fountain-heads of the social evil. Courtships, conducted as thousands of them are nowadays, can hardly fail to be productive of sorrow in many instances. The young man, under the impulse of passion, declares his love. Then, by oily words and artful caresses, he succeeds in winning the complete confidence of her whom he solemnly declares to be his choice from all the world. Step by step he steadily advances, until an immodest and sinful request is made. She at first refuses. Poor girl! Her sense of the pure

and the womanly is shocked at the
thought of committing an act out of the
holy bonds of wedlock which God intended only for the husband and wife.
"But," says her cruel tempter, "we are
just the same as married. We love each
other truly, and will soon be one legally.
What matters it to the world if we indulge our natural rights before the merely
formal requirements of the law are ful-
filled?" At last, after hours of entreaty
on his part and feverish anxiety on
hers; after hours of the most impolitic
and seductive physical contact—privileges that no decent man should ever ask
of any but a legal wife; and with his solemn promise of marriage oft repeated, she
yields, and her virtue—choicest possession of woman—is blighted forever!

Once successful, the tempter finds his
task less difficult a second time. A few
weeks of sinful pleasure, and to her chagrin and his fierce anger, the poor girl realizes that she is to become a mother.
She urges, pleads, implores immediate
marriage. He perhaps suggests abortion.
But noble woman, she scorns that wicked
and dangerous thought! And so, with-

out as much as a good-bye kiss, this foul youth takes the midnight train for parts unknown, and is soon looking for new worlds to conquer. She suffers the cruel consequences of the crime. The world frowns upon her, and casts her aside. In bitterness and tears, she treads the thorny pathway of life alone. Her merry laughter is turned to sobs. Her face of sunshine is covered with the clouds of despair and remorse. Yet love lingers— love for him to whom she gave her all. But how taunting, how heart-rending is such a love!

But how is it with our fine young man? The son of rich and cultured parents, per- haps, and possessed with a good supply of what the world calls "gall," he finds no difficulty in rising above the common herd and shining as a bright star in so- ciety wherever he goes. Perhaps he is soon in another marriage contract, which turns out like the first, and then another, and so on, until every moral fibre of his being is rotten with concupiscence and lust. Filthy fiend! So vile a wretch would seem almost too loathsome for use in paving the streets of hell! Dear reader, if *you* have ever been guilty of such a sin, I beg of you to repent in sack-cloth and ashes that God may forgive you. Otherwise you are lost forever, for the pearly gates of glory will never roll aside for such spotted sinners, unless they shall have first been washed in the blood of the Lamb.

I wish we could have an equal standard of morality to-day for man and woman. Why is it that one misstep on the part of woman is sufficient to make her an outcast from society, while her destroyer goes on to even higher planes of respectability? This is wrong. The same opprobrium should be heaped upon male and female in this matter. If this were the case, there would be comparatively few lapses from virtue. But as it is, the young man sins and pursues his course in society without a check, while the young woman is sneered at, tattled about, frozen down, and often driven into a life of shame.

Ella Wheeler Wilcox has given us a splendid pen-picture on this subject, as follows:

" There was a man, it was said, one time,
Who went astray in his youthful prime.
Can the brain keep cool and the heart be quiet,
When the blood's a river that's running riot?
And 'boys will be boys,' so the old folks say,
And 'the man is the better who's had his day.'
 * * * * * * *

The sinner reformed, and the preacher told
Of the prodigal son who came back to the fold.
And the Christian people threw open the door
With a warmer welcome than ever before.
Wealth and honor were his to command,
And a spotless woman gave him her hand.
The world strewed their pathway with flowers abloom,
Crying, ' God bless lady, and God bless groom.'

" There was a maiden who went astray,
In the golden dawn of life's young day.
She had more passion and heart than head,
And she followed blindly where fond love led.
And love unchecked is a dangerous guide
To wander at will by a fair girl's side.
 * * * * * *

The woman repented and turned from sin,
But no door was opened to let her in.
The preacher prayed that she might be forgiven,
But told her to look for mercy in heaven.
For this is the law of the earth, we know,
That the woman is scorned, while the man may go.
A brave man wedded her after all;
But the world said, frowning, ' We shall not call.' "

As if to prove the reality of this sad picture, the following note was received by the author shortly after the publication of her poem.

" Mrs. Ella Wheeler Wilcox,

Dear Madam: Will you let me thank you for the poem entitled ' The Two Sinners.' You who are so pure and charitable will understand the grateful feelings that one who was once a fallen woman must have toward you. I have found no mercy since I tried to regain my position among respectable people, and I despair of future hope. It may be that I shall return to my old life. Accept these few lines from one who is sincerely grateful. We may meet beyond the river. God bless you.

_____ _____ "

Another cause of unchastity—in fact a form of unchastity itself—is blackguardism. Men, young and old, indulge in telling lewd stories—fanning the flames of passion by the relation of filthy incidents. "Eminent professors (professors of vulgarity), some of our 'best' citizens, some church members, and a few preachers belong to this class," says Prof. Bryant. "They sit around in offices and stores where people have nothing to do, anyway, but to listen and laugh! And who now and then applaud with, 'that's a good 'un, ye got another?' 'That's a capper,' etc. These are the professors who are preparing our boys for saloon loafers and general bums, where they complete their course in all branches of whoredom. It makes me blush when I think how filthy men sometimes get. I have heard preachers tell stories so vulgar and dirty that I could almost smell the stench, and then go into the pulpit and point sinners to that spotless Lamb 'in whose mouth there was found no guile.' Is it any wonder that 'there are no Josephs nowadays?' These vulgar stories would corrupt the morals of angels. Jesus said, 'From the abundance of the heart the mouth speaketh.' This is true. These stories are but the effervescence of the boiling soul. From a pure heart no such can come. This is the junior department of the great university which prepares men for the work of ruining homes and blighting the lives of the innocent. From this they enter into training for all branches of crime. Its graduates are doing a big work. They are found on almost every line of railroad from Maine to California. They appear in the capacity of 'mashers,' and they are well skilled in their art. They try to 'make a mash' on every young girl traveling alone. They capture many of them by their oily tongues, and sometimes by drugs. Many brothels are supplied by them with inmates. There the poor victim is kept until ruined by disease, when she is turned into the street to become one of the lowest order of prostitutes—to rot and die. Then her place is filled by a newly-made victim.

"Talk of social purity, but you can never see it until you have dried up the fountain at the source of the stream—the fountain of corruption that flows from the mouths of vulgar blackguards. No man who will sit around and tell vulgar stories is fit to be received into decent society. The church should withdraw from him, and social ethics should say to him, 'Stand outside until you have been cleansed from your filth.' This is the only way to save a sinking race; it is the only balm that will heal the cankered soul; the only remedy that will kill the cancer which is eating at the vitals of life. Let us stop this vulgarity if we can, or soon wreck and ruin will mark the end of such a course. We are all out upon the ocean of life, sailing on toward eternity's fair haven of rest. Let us shun the reefs and rocks on which other barks have been broken. Do not look upon adultery, or adulterous conversation, as honorable in man. It is not. It is ruinous. It poisons the mind. It takes from his nature all that is holy and pure, and leaves him a moral wreck. Do not tread the adulterous road yourself, nor walk with those who do. Treat an adulterous man as you would treat his fallen sister—sever your acquaintance with him until he has reformed: then help him up the hill of life. To foster a licentious man in society is like fondling a viper in the bosom."

It is a deplorable fact that many men who would scorn to lie or steal, considering these misdemeanors as they should frightful sins, yet do not regard it very wicked to step over the lines of the strictest chastity occasionally. But let us see what the Word of God says.

In Exodus 20:14, we read: "Thou shalt not commit adultery." This was one of the Ten Commandments, and precedes those bearing on lying and theft.

In Galatians 5:19-21, we read: "Now the works of the flesh are manifest, which are these: adultery, fornication, uncleanness, lasciviousness, idolatry, witchcraft, hatred, variance, emulations, wrath, strife, seditions, heresies, envyings, murders, drunkenness, revellings, and such like, of the which I tell you before, as I have also told you in time past, that they which do such things shall not inherit the kingdom of heaven." Here the apostle Paul places adultery, fornication, and kindred crimes at the head of the list.

Turn to Matt. 5:27, 28, and read the words of Jesus in his great Sermon on the Mount, which contains many of the fundamental principles of Christianity and the higher life: "Ye have heard that it hath been said by them of old time, Thou shalt not commit adultery. But I say unto you, That whosoever looketh on a woman to lust after her, hath committed adultery with her already in his heart."

Once more, read thoughtfully Rev. 21:8: "But the fearful, and unbelieving, and the abominable, and murderers, and whoremongers, and sorcerers, and idolaters, and all liars, shall have their part in the lake which burneth with fire and brimstone, which is the second death."

Take your reference Bible, and, if you
desire to trace the matter further, you
can easily find scores of passages along
the same line. God condemns unchastity
in all its forms. He never intended that
his children should exercise their sexual
privileges outside of consecrated wedlock,
and the man who does it, young or old,
saint or sinner, blights his purity every
time, and forfeits his right to the Tree of
Life. The laws of man are also against
the social evil generally, and ought always
to be so, for it is an evil dangerous alike
to the individual and the state.

"In looking through the pages of history," says Dr. Dio Lewis, "we see the
fairest societies corrupted by libertinism,
until at last they drop to pieces from very
rottenness. The Saturnalian orgies of
ancient Rome were the efficient cause of
her downfall. Epicures in vice were not
satisfied with ordinary crimes, but sought
out every low and disgusting form of lust,
to give the zest of novelty to its indulgence. Nero took emetics after a full
meal that he might renew the gratification of his gluttony, and excited his
palled senses with love-philters that he

might plunge into fresh debaucheries.
The closest ties of blood were no protection; incest was common. Caligula committed this horrible crime with all his sisters. Fathers violated the honor of their
own daughters. Who can tell from what
polluted stream were filled the veins of
that Italian father whose unnatural heart
was pierced in later days by the dagger of
Beatrice Cenci?

"We read with a shiver of disgust how
the Empress Messalina pitted herself
against a most notorious courtesan, and
outdid her in the number of men she ad-
mitted in one night to her embraces. He
who declared that Cæsar's wife must be
above suspicion, like many a late Cæsar,
considered his right to a monopoly of the
vices beyond all question, and in the lack
of more new worlds to conquer applied
himself to the general overthrow of femi-
nine virtue. Bacchus and Venus were
the gods to whose worship every instinct
of decency was sacrificed. In certain
temples, after the religious ceremonies
were ended, the lights were put out, and
indiscriminate license prevailed. Helio-
gabulus drove naked through the streets

of Rcme, attended by a crowd of his favorite women in the same condition. The wife of Augustus, in order to preserve her influence with her husband, sought out young girls for his lecherous gratification, an example that was afterward followed at the corrupt French court by Madame de Maintenon toward her royal lover. In Greece, corruption was no less universal, though it was marked with a semblance of refinement. The famous courtesans of the State were also its most gifted women. Aspasia, the mistress of Pericles, was the admiration of all Greece. Socrates, the teacher of morals, was licentious in the extreme!

"A glance at Egpyt reveals a like state of morals. The huge pyramid of Cheops was built by the lovers of king Ptolemy's daughter, its height attesting the number of her prostitutions. The story of Cleopatra is too well known to need more than a reference. She personified the spirit of the age as she stepped from the rich tapestry in which she had been rolled, and, all drenched with perfume, stood out before the king, nude, beautiful, and shameless. In modern Europe, the cor-

ruption of France in the reigns just pre-
ceding the Revolution is well known. A
virtuous woman was obliged to apologize
for her eccentricity. Madame de Sevigne
records with equanimity in the one case,
and pleasure in the other, the devotion
of her husband and son to the notorious
Ninon de l'Enclos, a woman who kept up
her prostitutions to so advanced an age
that her own grandson fell in love with
her, and killed himself when told of the
relationship between them. In Italy, the
vices of the Borgias and the Medicis were
proverbial. Jane I, queen of Naples, or-
ganized brothels, and they were established in various cities of Italy and
France. In seeking the causes for the
overthrow of these different nations, or
the social revolutions that have agitated
them, we invariably find that the licentiousness of their people has bred decay
within them, and led to their decline and
fall."

The suicide of Boulanger at the grave
of his mistress is yet fresh in the memory
of France. And in the winter of 1891-92,
the good people of Iowa were much
chagrined over the conduct of two of

their representatives in the State Legislature, who were caught visiting a house of ill-fame, and loudly written up by the daily papers. Thus an uncontrolled sexual appetite corrupts the brightest stars of genius and good fortune as well as the lowest thugs of slumdum.

The sexual appetite controlled is all right. It is that without which a man is nothing. It is no disgrace to be richly endowed with sexual power, but on the other hand a choice blessing. But it must be managed by reason, controlled by the will, or, like the cheerful fire that warms us, it may ruin all in one brief hour.

"But," says one, "nature has given us the sexual appetite, and it must be gratified."

Very well; select a pure and devoted woman, make her your wife, and then with temperance proceed to gratify both your own and her appetite. There is no wrong in this, and it saves multitudes from evil, and spurs them forward to the highest achievements in life. But unless you are willing to enter into matrimony, it is mean and unmanly for you to talk about gratifying your sexual nature. It is a mistake, anyway, to say that you *must*. The ablest physicians say that it is not essential to good health, usefulness, and success in life. And the brilliant achievements of some of the world's purest and most gifted characters who have lived and died single prove the correctness of this theory. "I, in connection with many of our best and wisest men who have given the subject a lifetime's most earnest consideration," says Dr. Guernsey, of Philadelphia, "hold that for a young man whose early education has been carefully looked to, and consequently whose mind has not been debased by vile practices, it is no more impossible mentally, or injurious physically, to preserve his chastity than to refrain from yielding to any other of the innumerable temptations with which his life is beset. And every year of voluntary chastity renders the task easier by mere force of habit."

"A mischievous notion has obtained in the world that continence is injurious," says Dr. Dio Lewis. "Some physicians teach this. Books are written to prove it. 'Supporting themselves on the one hand

with the imperious nature of the generative instinct, they sustain the opinion
that man cannot restrain himself by the
sole force of his will. On the other hand,
admitting that God has made the regular
accomplishment of the organic functions
a condition of health and life, they say
that the continent man does injury to
himself.' The authority of Hippocrates,
Galen, and other ancient physicians, is
quoted to prove that sexual abstinence
produces certain diseases; that it exposes
man to satyriasis and impotence, and
woman to uterine furor, nymphomania,
or hysteria. All this affords the immoral
a ready excuse for their debauchery. If it
were true, we should have nothing more
to say—we would give up our fight against
vice, and withdraw our condemnation of
sexual relations outside of marriage. But
examining science and questioning phys-
iology on this subject will readily enable
us to refute all such arguments. *The laws
of nature are always in harmony with the
precepts of morality.* When scientific re-
searches chance to lay down a law which
is contrary to morality and religion, they
should be distrusted, for in such teach-

ings there is always concealed error. Beyond doubt, as men now live, continence is almost impossible. They drug themselves with tobacco, and excite themselves with wine. They enervate their powers in heated rooms, and read books which arouse lascivious desires. Naturally, sexual passion attacks them; and if it be refused gratification, they become fevered and restless, and declare that health demands frequent intercourse and suffers without it.

"But it is *not* a physiological necessity. Under certain conditions, absolute continence is consistent with the highest health during the whole lifetime. To attain this, however, one must live in perfect accordance with hygienic laws; he cannot expect to suppress one vice and yield to another. A boatman in training for a race, a pedestrian for a walking tour, a prize-fighter for a tussle, will all tell you that in order to have their powers at the best, they must abstain from sexual intercourse and every form of intemperance. They will say that after the first few days of abstinence they ceased to be tormented by any unlawful desires, and were stronger, firmer, and more sure of themselves than ever before in their lives. As for the instances of disease that have been mentioned, modern medical observation has exculpated continence from the charges brought against it as their primary cause. 'It is easy to demonstrate that the examples reported are rare exceptions; that the individuals attacked had peculiar predispositions to the diseases which affected them. Many more hysterical and insane persons are found in houses of prostitution than in convents.' Let it be understood that we advocate absolute continence, except in peculiar and individual cases. We merely wish to state in the most positive manner that it neither injures the health nor abridges the longevity of those upon whom duty imposes its observance.''

It is said of Sir Isaac Newton, the great scholar and scientist, who lived and died a bachelor, that on his death-bed he informed his physician that he had never lost a drop of semen in his life. And yet many men give way to passion and sin. What a fearful thing to do! Not only is your own character stained, but that of

her whom you seduce. It is a dual sin.
Multitudes of innocent girls thus lose their
most priceless possession—virginity.
What man would care to wed the girl who
had, in an evil hour, given to another this
choicest gift? Would you? Oh, no! Then
how dare you presume to make advances
so ruinous toward any pure girl?

"Well, then, what would be wrong in
visiting those who have fallen, and to
whom virtue is no more a golden word?"
says another.

The wrong is just the same in principle
—the one is fornication, and so is the
other. But the latter might be infinitely
worse in practice. Listen to the wise man
on this point: "For the lips of a strange woman (prostitute) drop as a honeycomb, and
her mouth is smoother than oil. But her
end is bitter as wormwood, sharp as a
two-edged sword. Her feet go down to
death; her steps take hold on hell. Remove thy way far from her, and come not
nigh the door of her house, lest thou give
thine honour unto others, and thy years
unto the cruel; lest strangers be filled with
thy wealth, and thy labours be in the
house of a stranger; and thou mourn at

the last, when thy flesh and thy body are consumed." (Prov. 5: 3, 4, 5, 8, 9, 10, 11).

Illicit sexual intercourse is not only dangerous to the soul, but also to the body. I want to be understood here. The man who visits a whore to gratify his lust does so at the risk of his life. "Many promising youths," says Dr. Guernsey, "just as they are blossoming into the pride of early manhood, begin to indulge in sexual thoughts, and to allow these thoughts to influence their minds until they commit some of the evils to which perverted and unchaste passions lead them. If this evil be masturbation, then they are on the direct road to ruin. If it be the commission of sexual intercourse with women, their ruin is still more certain, and in the latter case they are exposed to one of the worst poisons that can possibly infect the human race. I do not overdraw the picture when I declare that *millions of human beings die annually from the effects of poison contracted in this way*, in some form of suffering or other; for, by insinuating its effects into and poisoning the whole man, it complicates various disorders and

renders them incurable. When gonorrhea is contracted, although frequently
suppressed by local treatment in the form
of injections, it is never perfectly cured
thereby. No, the hidden poison runs on
for a life-time, producing strictures, dy-
suria, gleet, and kindred diseases; finally,
in old men, a horrible prostatitis results
from which the balance of one's life is
rendered miserable indeed. If inflamma-
tion of the lungs supervenes, there is often
a translation of the virus to these vital
organs, causing what is termed 'plastic
pneumonia,' where one lobule after another becomes gradually sealed up, until
nearly the whole of both lungs becomes
impervious to air, and death results from
asphyxia.

"This horrible infection sometimes becomes engrafted upon other acute diseases
when lingering disorders follow, causing
years of misery, and only terminating in
death. If real syphilis, in the form of
chancre, should be contracted, and in
that form suppressed, we have buboes
often of a malignant type, ulceration of
the penis, and a loss of some portion of
this member. Sometimes the poison

attacks the throat, causing most destructive alterations therein. Sometimes it seizes upon the nasal bones, resulting in their entire destruction and an awful disfigurement of the face. Sometimes it ultimates itself in the ulceration and destruction of other osseous tissues in different portions of the body. Living examples of these facts are too frequently witnessed in the streets of any large city. Young men marrying with the slightest taint of this poison in the blood will surely transmit the disease to their children. Thousands of abortions transpire every year from this cause alone, the poison being so destructive as to kill the child *in utero*, before it is matured for birth; and even if the child be born alive, it is liable to break down with the most loathsome disorders of some kind, and die during dentition; the few that survive this period are short-lived and are unhealthy so long as they do live. The first unchaste connection of a man with a woman may be attended with a contamination entailing upon him a life of suffering, and even death itself. There is no safety among impure or loose women, whether in private homes or in

the best regulated houses of ill-fame.
Even in Paris, where, after women have
been carefully examined and pronounced
free from any infecting condition, the first
man who visits one of them often carries
away a deadly enemy in his blood, which
had lurked in concealment beyond the
keen eye of the inspector. A young man,
or a man at any age, is in far greater
danger amidst company of this stamp than
he would be with a clean conscience and
pure character in the midst of the wildest
forest, full of all manner of poisonous
serpents and wild beasts of every description. A knowledge of the above
facts should be enough to chill the first
impulse, and to make any man who respects his own well-being turn away and
flee from the destruction that awaits him."

Speaking of venereal diseases, the author
of a good old medical work entitled "The
Family Doctor" says: "Had we been
able to satisfy our conscience in doing so, we
would have avoided all reference to these
truly loathsome diseases, which present
an awful illustration of the scripture,
'The way of the transgressor is hard.'
As we write we have before the vivid eye

of our memory a series of facts which might almost make our ears tingle. A young man connected with a family of the highest respectability early in life indulged in the sin which brought on syphilis. Much labor and expense led, as it was believed, to a full cure, and after a few years he married a most estimable lady of wealth and beauty, entered an honorable profession, and by his piety and benevolence rose to high esteem in the community. The middle period of life arrived, his wealth increased, and a large and beautiful family of children surrounded him. Disease attacked him, and physicians at length were compelled to tell him that he suffered from uneradicated and incurable disease *arising from the sins of his youth.* In a state of chagrin and grief which the pen cannot describe, he soon after ended the mournful tragedy by death. YOUNG MEN, BEWARE!

"*Syphilis, or pox,*" says this writer, "must not be neglected, unless the patient would die. The history of this disease and the mischief it has done in the world for many centuries are truly terrific. Almost imperceptible in its origin, it corrupts the

whole body, makes the very air offensive
to surrounding friends, and lays multitudes literally to rot in the grave. It
commences in one part of the body and
usually, in more or less degree, extends to
the whole system, and is said by most
eminent physicians to be a morbid poison,
having the power of extending itself to
every part of the body into which it is infused, and to other persons with whom it
in any way comes in contact, so that
even its moisture, communicated by linen
or otherwise, may corrupt those who un-
fortunately touch it. Innumerable remedies have been prescribed for it, but it is
difficult to say when it is really cured.
Indeed, some very wise men have doubted
whether it is ever radically removed.
Whatever shame may be felt by the unhappy patient, if there be a proper regard
for life, to say nothing of the interests of
society, the best accessible physician will
be consulted and his counsels most carefully adhered to."

Yes, truly, unchastity is burdened with
sorrows of every character. Why will
men go on so thoughtlessly and wickedly
in this forbidden way! And yet they do.

The press is full of sad stories illustrating to what desperate ends a depraved sexual appetite will drive both men and women. Some are brought to punishment in this world; some are not. But all will be brought to judgment at the last day.

I want to quote one of these tales of woe just as it appeared in a Kansas City daily, March 11, 1892. Hundreds like it might be culled from the columns of our leading journals everywhere. Here it is, with all its harrowing details. May its perusal call forth a solemn pledge on the part of every reader never to be guilty himself of any unchastity, God helping him, but on the other hand to live a pure life, and do all in his power to assist others to do likewise:

James Crantz, the Salina horse trader, has been declared to be the murderer of Grace Ellen Barber. After balloting five hours, the jury in the criminal court at Liberty found him guilty of murder in the second degree. A sentence of twenty-five years in the penitentiary was made. It is not probable that an appeal will be taken as Crantz is almost penniless. The last argument was ended yesterday about one o'clock and the jury was charged.

The first ballot stood one for acquittal,
three for hanging and eight for murder in
the second degree. After a long discussion
of the evidence, the jury made a compromise verdict. The sheriff was on the
point of adjourning court, when at six
o'clock a knocking was heard on the door
of the jury room. The twelve men were
brought out and polled by Clerk Reed.
Prosecuting Attorney John Dougherty
was not in the room, so the announcement
of the verdict was delayed until he could
be called. Nobody spoke, and the silence
was oppressive.

WOULD RATHER BE HANGED.

When the words of the sentence were
read, perspiration gathered in beads on the
murderer's forehead and a sickly smile
played on his lips.

"I'd rather be hung than sent to the
penitentiary," was the only remark he
made.

The jury was discharged and Crantz
was taken back to the dungeon, which
constitutes Clay County's jail. The murder was an unusually brutal one. Crantz
was a horse trader in Solomon, Kas., and
had a family. Mrs. Grace Ellen Barber
was a woman past middle life, but wayward. Her husband was separated from
her. They came to Kansas City—Crantz
says that they met here, but this was dis-

proved—and went to a lodging house kept by Le Prise, on Ninth Street, a few doors east of Wyandotte Street, where they rented a room under the name of "Mr. and Mrs Nelson." They remained there a week.

THE FATAL TRIP TO RANDOLPH.

One Saturday evening, late in April, they left the house, saying that they were going to Kansas City, Kas., to live. They went across the river to Harlem and there bought tickets to Liberty. They boarded the four o'clock Burlington train, and passengers say they were quarreling. The woman wept. At Randolph they left the car and started east along the tracks. R. H. McCormack followed them and heard Crantz abuse the woman. Other persons saw them take that last walk. Early the next morning—it was Sunday—two young men out hunting found the woman's dead body. It was lying in a ravine on top of a very high bluff, reached by a precipitous path. Around the woman's throat was a handkerchief. A piece of wood was thrust through it and it was twisted deep into the flesh. There was the mark of a blow on the then bloated and discolored face. All day long the body lay on the rocks awaiting the coming of Coroner Rice, who did not arrive until sunset. An

inquest was held. The verdict said that
a murder had been done, and the murderer
was unknown, and with unseemly haste
the body was put in a pine box and buried.

BETRAYED BY THE CLOTHING.

That Sunday morning Crantz took
some of the clothing which had belonged
to the woman, then dead, and left it with
a colored woman named Sallie Pleasanton
in Harlem. For three days Constable
Will McCoy shadowed the house.
Wednesday night the murderer returned,
by some strange fate, to get the clothing,
and was caught. The woman had had
some money, but none was found in the
clothing. After the arrest the body of the
garroted woman was exhumed and identi-
fied as that of Mrs. Barber, alias Nelson.
Crantz stoutly denied the awful crime,
but the chain of circumstantial evidence
was convicting.

"It was the strongest case of the kind
ever made," said Chief of Police Speers.

Crantz' wife, to whom he had been
unfaithful, now lives with a child in this
city. Crantz says he will not appeal from
the sentence.

And now let me give one more incident,
illustrative of the foulest kind of work in
which the devil can induce his imps to
engage—that of seducing poor girls under

the garb of affection and the promise of marriage. I quote from Prof. Bryant's lecture on "Social Purity:"

"Some years ago there lived a family in one of the thriving villages of the West, whose brightest star was Viola, a charming maiden of only fourteen summers. She was one of the fairest of the fair, and of rare intelligence. While yet in this tender age, she was courted by Willie, who, in point of wealth and culture, was her equal. From courtship strong ties of affection grew. She had promised to be his wife. She honored and trusted him; and in a time when her own passions were at their highest tide, she encountered the force of his. With a solemn promise of marriage upon his lips, he obtained her consent to sacrifice virtue to gratify lust. A victory once gained was easily gained again. With virtue lost and defeat sustained, she had lost all power to resist him; yet she hoped that all would be well.

"Alas! the day of sorrow came. To her it was known that she must become a mother. She trustingly told Willie of her sad condition, and urged a speedy marriage. The day was set, but came and passed, and Willie was not there. He was gone from her forever to meet her face no more until at the Judgment Bar of God. Frantic with grief, she went into her room and wrote an account of the whole affair. Then, leaving it on the table, when day was lost in midnight's darkest hour, she quietly left the room and went out to wander in the cold world alone, until worn out and broken down in health and heart she should resign her body back to dust from whence it came and her spirit to God who gave it. How many doors have thus been closed while father and mother are quietly sleeping and dreaming not of ill? God alone can tell.

"Many months and years passed by. Father or mother made no effort to save the lost child. Her room for awhile was draped in mourning (they mourned for her as dead); then it was lit with the cheerful light again; but never by the sweet smiles, nor made happy by the cheerful songs of poor lost Viola. They were hushed forever there. At two different times a letter came—one to father's address and one to mother's. They knew the handwriting; it was that of their lost child. They would forget her. They cared not to know her tale of sorrow and of shame. Her letters were unopened and unread. How many tear stains, how many pleadings for mercy and deliverance, how many prayers for forgiveness those unbroken seals contained, we shall never know.

"At last her lifeless body was found in an alley of one of the large cities, where all kinds of vice and crime are common, and on her person was found a simple note which read: 'Dear Papa and Mamma: I forgive you both. If you ever see Willie, tell him that poor Viola died praying for him.' Yes, true love cannot die. While life on earth remained, she loved him through all her shame. I am not here to preach her funeral, but I will say that if there is justice in the great beyond, when that young man is reeking amidst the flames of hell, those bright eyes which he dimmed with sorrow here and bathed in briny tears for shame, will be looking out from the windows of heaven upon his doomed soul, and with those sweet lips that he pressed

with unholy kiss she will say to him, 'O
Willie! I forgave you, but God would not.'

"It is not always that parents abandon
their deceived and ruined daughter to her
fate, but it is sometimes so. The door is
ever open to the returning prodigal son,
and the fatted calf surely is killed when
he comes; but it is not always so with the
wayward daughter. The friends seldom, if
ever, make merry with her. May heaven
be more merciful to us than we have been
to poor fallen woman! Remember that
she is of our race and God loves her still;
for her the heavens bled through His
lovely Son. Then for her shall we not
shed a tear? Be we *men*, or be we *demons?*
Our lives shall answer best."

I believe that the social evil, with its
kindred sins, can be largely cured if men
will do their duty. Few women would
ever fall from virtue were it not for the
satanic intrigues of passionate men. And
if society were consistent, there are but
few fallen women who could not be redeemed. The crying need of this age is
an equal standard of morals for both
sexes. And for this I trust every reader
of these lines will fight to the best of his

ability. The adulterous man is just as much a sinner as the adulterous woman, and often much more so. If it is wrong for your sister to fornicate, it is wrong for you. If it is a heinous crime for your wife to grant her favors to another man, it is equally so for you to give to another that which, according to the laws of God and man, belongs only to the queen of your home and heart. Many married men, when they go down to the great city on business, think it little harm to spend a night or two with a harlot. But if their wives should be guilty just once of an act like that, they would consider it sufficient cause for a divorce forthwith. And so it would be. But why such a distinction in morals?

Again, if we would cure the social evil, we must be willing to help the truly penitent to a higher life. The disposition so prevalent nowadays to kick every person that's down is not manly, much less Christian. We should be willing to open the doors of our churches and our homes to every prodigal sister as well as prodigal brother when they come with truly repentant hearts. In this men must take the lead, for, strange as it truly appears, women will not. One of the bitterest enemies of fallen woman is woman un-fallen. It ought not to be so, but it is. So men must take the initial in the reformation of their lost sisters. Hate the sin, but love the sinner. Treat her decently and kindly. Be the personification of purity, courtesy, and genuine manliness before her, and you will do more to save her than all the frowns and sneers that could be heaped upon her already burdened character in a thousand years. The Lord Jesus Christ had tender compassion on the penitent prostitute. On one occasion, when He was at meat, a poor, sinful, but sorrowful, woman washed His feet with tears and wiped them with her hair. To her the ever-loving and merciful Saviour said, "Thy faith hath saved thee; go in peace." (Luke 7:36-50.) On another occasion the hypocritical Pharisees brought a woman to Him for judgment who had been taken in the very act of adultery. To their amazement and utter chagrin He said, when asked if she should not be stoned, "He that is without sin among you, let him cast the first stone." Immediately her persecutors slunk away for shame, and Jesus said, "Woman, where are those thine accusers? hath no man condemned thee?" With penitent voice the poor sinner replied, "No man, Lord." And then what did Jesus do? Turn his back upon her, and, like modern society, say, "Begone, you nasty thing?" Oh, no! Jesus said, "Neither do I condemn thee; go, and sin no more." (Jno. 8:3-11.) Let this spirit once take possession of every church and moral society to-day, and a long stride toward the cure of prostitution in all its forms will have been taken. Observe the Golden Rule in this as in all other things.

By way of reiteration, let me impress upon you, dear reader, these plain points:

First, adultery and fornication, in deed or in thought, are sins. If you have ever been guilty of their commission in the past, resolve now that you will never be again.

Second, illicit sexual intercourse shall be regarded as just as grave an offense in male as in female. You should no more

yield to the impulses of lust than your
wife or sister.

Third, aside from its moral phases, visiting a house of prostitution is a most
dangerous business. One trip of this
kind might cost you your life. But even
if it did not cut your own days short, it
might bring upon your wife and offspring
untold suffering. A man of my knowledge
once visited a harlot at the time of his
wife's pregnancy, when it was impossible,
I suppose, for her, poor slave, to accept-
ably gratify the carnal desires of her liege
lord. He caught "the bad disease," returned to his wife's bed and gave it to
her, and the result was the birth of a
scabby child, which lived but a short time
and died. What must a mother in heaven
think of such a human dog?

Fourth, to seduce a pure girl is a crime
that should be regarded beneath the dignity of a barbarian, much less of a cultured man living in a land of Bibles
and Sunday-schools. The consequences
of such a deed are followed by such heart-
rending regrets and experiences of woe
that the very thought of sexual gratification outside of holy, happy wedlock

should fill every true man's soul with disgust for libertinism, and with an intense longing after a higher life.

Fifth, to escape a sad result, a wise man will avoid its causes. "An ounce of prevention is better than a pound of cure." Steer clear of bad habits, bad company, bad thoughts. Keep away from the dance, the low-down theatre, and the seductive influences of midnight courtships as at present carried on.

Sixth, look with as much disgust and pity upon the male adulterer and fornicator as upon the female. When they repent and try to live purer lives, be as ready to receive one as the other.

In short, BE MANLY. Live on the sweet, high plane of purity. For all such virtue has a great work to do, and will pay abundant wages in health, happiness, and life eternal.

"We live in deeds, not years; in thoughts, not breaths;
In feelings, not in figures on a dial.
We should count time by heart-throbs. He most lives,
Who thinks most, feels the noblest, acts the best."
—*Bailey*

CHAPTER VIII.

THE SECRET VICE; OR, THE UNNATURAL SIN OF MASTURBATION.

A Chicago medical professor is authority for the statement that ninety-nine per cent. of the males of this age, and twenty-five to thirty per cent. of the females, are guilty, at some time in life, of practicing the secret vice, or the unnatural sin of masturbation. Whether the professor is correct or not in his estimate, I do not know—nobody knows; for owing to its secrecy and peculiar subtlety, it is impossible to concisely tabulate the extent of the ravages of this sin. But that it is an evil of alarming magnitude all careful observers are agreed, and hence I feel it to be my duty to speak, and speak plainly, concerning this.

There is a flood of literature on the subject to-day, but from the greater bulk of it I pray that the youths of this country may be delivered. Hundreds of medical sharks, posing as the friends of suffering men, are getting rich from the sale of their contemptible publications and abominable drugs. In one column of a New York paper recently I counted eleven different advertisements from this class of fleecers. One of them commended a certain wonderful book very highly, which if the poor fellow who was suffering from "youthful indiscretions," "lost manhood," etc., would read, he would learn the way to health and happiness again. It is a book that sells for $1. The publishers claim that it has had the remarkably large sale of one million copies, I believe. I sent for the work and received a little volume made up quite largely of accounts of the author's "brilliant achievements" in curing the diseases of men, together with many scary statements as to the terribleness of neglecting immediate treatment at the hands of one who held a "gold medal" or two for his discoveries, and who always regarded the letters of his correspondents as "sacredly confidential," but who would pay no attention to any communications unless they contained an introductory fee of FIVE DOLLARS! Ah, yes! The fee was the big item, the end most of all desired on the part of this would-be benefactor of his race.

Some of these scoundrels will reply in such a way as to almost frighten the uninitiated into spasms. A physician in Iowa told me that he once answered one of these advertisements just to see what reply he would get. He used a plain sheet of paper and a yellow envelope, and wrote as poorly as he could. He represented himself to be suffering from seminal losses, and sought help from a great (?) Clark or Nassau Street specialist. The specialist replied promptly, and told his correspondent that he could detect in his very handwriting the fact that he was in a very dangerous condition etc. He could cure him, however. The charges would be "reasonable"—only "fifteen dollars down, and then five dollars per month until cured." Yes, there it is, the old game of *dollar, dollar*. Nearly every newspaper abounds with advertisements of this character, designed to catch the unwary.

But whatever else may be said, the fact

that these quacks catch thousands of the unwary every year is pretty good proof that the evil of which we speak is exceedingly common. The gentler sex is by no means free from the fearful clutches of this ferocious enemy of body, soul and spirit; but so much more common among males than females is it that I regard masturbation as peculiarfy a startling sin of the sterner sex.

The nature of this terrible practice is too well known to need much description. Suffice it to say here that masturbation consists in " exciting the genitals by mechanical means of some sort." In other words, *playing with the privates*—one of the most loathsome and damaging acts in which it is possible for a son of Adam to engage. And yet it is one of the most generally practiced sins of the age.

" Self-abuse, or masturbation," says one eminent medical writer, " is probably the most common, and certainly the most damaging, of all forms of sexual vice. There are, oi course, no accurate statistics wherewith the extent to which this vice prevails may be determined; but there can be no doubt that the evil far exceeds

in magnitude the estimates of those whose
opportunities for observation have not
been such as to give them an adequate
idea of this dreadful physical and moral
blight."

"Books and pamphlets on this subject
in great numbers for a score of years
past," says another, "have been printed
and widely disseminated, and yet, if we
are to believe those physicians and educa-
tors whose paths lie across the records of
deeds done in secret, masturbation is as
prevalent—and perhaps more so—in our
day as in days gone by. In schools and
out of schools, females as well as males—
married as well as single—are to be found
those bearing the imprint of the great
wrong done their souls by this low, de-
basing, unmanly, cowardly practice of
self-abuse. The extent of the vice cannot
be ascertained—its nature prevents it;
but that it is, in connection with sexual
excess, lowering and undermining the
health, strength and ability of thousands
of the young who otherwise would make
their mark in the world is palpable to all
who possess the skill to rightly judge from
plainly visible effects back to legitimate

causes. The practice of this vice, so common among boys, and not very uncommon among girls, is one of the great reasons why they never attain distinction in their educational endeavors, or attain high positions in the world's department of work.

"In my lectures to men only in different educational institutions in the United States—in universities and colleges east and west"— said the noted revivalist J. V. Updike, in one of his addresses, "I presume I have counseled with at least one hundred young men in the past month—from the age of twenty-one down —in regard to this fearful practice of masturbation. Some told me that they commenced the practice at the early age of six and kept it up, not knowing that it was harmful until they heard my lecture on the subject."

There is great need of information along this line to-day. The masses are practically in dense ignorance regarding the real character, extent and injuriousness of this vile habit. We have in the neighborhood of 100,000 preachers in this country, but very few of them ever say

anything on this subject. It is largely
owing to its delicate nature, I presume.
Society forbids that a minister should
speak of such matters, at least before a
mixed audience. Then many are not
posted on the nature and magnitude of
the evil. Too many clergymen spend
their lives in the realm of theory, scarcely
ever coming down to the practical. This
is all wrong. This is a world of ignorance,
and sin, and shame. Teachers of religion
must not take too much for granted with
reference to the personal purity of their
constituency, but freely and fearlessly
come down to every-day life, and throw out
such warnings, and point out such paths of
duty, as shall save the individual in all his
parts.

It is probable that some writers have
over-estimated the prevalence and evil
effects of the secret vice. But on the
other hand, parents, public teachers, and
even many physicians, have greatly under-
estimated. Certain it is that the best authorities in the world are now speaking,
and that with no uncertain sound, on this
subject. In an address on "Idiocy and
Insanity," delivered before the Massa-

chusetts senate, Dr. S. G. Howe used the following forcible paragraphs:

"There is another vice—a monster so hideous in mien, so disgusting in feature, and altogether so beastly and loathsome, that in very shame and cowardice it hides its head by day, and, vampire-like, sucks the very life blood from its victims by night (and it may commit more direct ravages upon the strength and reason of its victims than even intemperance), and that vice is SELF-ABUSE. One would fain be spared the sickening task of dealing with this disgusting subject, but as he who would exterminate the wild beasts that ravage his fields must not fear to enter their dark and noisome dens and drag them out of their lair, so he who would rid humanity of a pest must not shrink from dragging it from its hiding places to perish in the light of day. If men deified him who delivered Lerna from its hydra, and canonized him who delivered Ireland from its serpents, what should they do for one who could extirpate this monster vice? What is the ravage of fields, the slaughter of flocks, or even the poison of serpents, compared with that

pollution of body and soul, that utter ex-
tinction of reason, and that degradation
of beings made in God's own image, to
a condition which it would be an insult to
the animals to call beastly, and which is
so often the consequence of excessive
indulgence in this vice?

"It cannot be that such loathsome
wrecks of humanity as men and women
reduced to drivelling idiocy by this cause
should be permitted to float upon the tide
of life without some useful purpose; and the
only one we can conceive of is that of
awful beacons to make others avoid, as
they would eschew moral pollution and
death, the course which leads to such
reason. This may seem extravagant
language, but there can be no exaggeration, for there can be no adequate description even, of the horrible condition
to which men and women are reduced by
the practice. There are among those enumerated in this report some who were
once considered young gentlemen and
ladies, but who are now moping idiots—
idiots of the lowest kind; lost to all reason,
to all moral sense, to all shame; idiots
who have but one thought, one wish, one

passion, and that is the further indulgence in the habit which has loosed the silver cord even in early youth—which has already wasted, and, as it were, dissolved the fibrous part of their bodies, and utterly extinguished their minds. In such extreme cases there is nothing left to appeal to—absolutely less than there is in dogs and horses, for they may be acted upon by fear of punishment; but these poor creatures are beyond all fear and all hope. They cumber the earth awhile, living masses of corruption. If only such lost and helpless wretches existed it would be a duty to cover them charitably with the veil of concealment, and hide them from the public eye as things too nauseous to be seen; but alas, they are only the *most* unfortunate members of a large class. They have sunk down in the abyss toward which thousands are tending. The vice that has shorn these poor creatures of the fairest attributes of humanity is acting upon others, in a less degree indeed, but still very injuriously, enervating the body, weakening the mind and polluting the soul.

"A knowledge of the extent to which

this vice prevails would astonish and shock many. It is indeed a pestilence that walks in darkness, because, while it saps and weakens all the higher qualities of the mind, it so strengthens low cunning and deceit that the victim goes on in his habit unsuspected, until arrested by some one whose practiced eye reads his sin in the very means he takes to conceal it, or until all sense of shame is forever lost in the night of idiocy with which his day so early closes. Many a child who confides everything else to a loving parent conceals this practice in his innermost heart. Sons and daughters who dutifully, conscientiously and religiously confess themselves to father, mother or priest, on every other subject, never allude to this. Nay, they try to cheat and deceive by false appearances; for as against this darling sin, duty, conscience, and religion are all nothing. They even think to cheat God, or cheat themselves into the belief that He who is of purer eyes than to behold iniquity can still regard their sin with favor. Many a fond parent looks with wondering anxiety upon the puny frame, the feeble purpose, the fitful hu-

mors of a dear child, and after trying all
other remedies to restore him to vigor of
body and vigor of mind, goes journeying
about from place to place, hoping to leave
the offending cause behind, while the
victim hugs the disgusting serpent closely
in his bosom—conceals it carefully in his
vestment.

" The evils which this sinful habit works
in a direct and positive manner are not so
appreciable, perhaps, as those which it
effects in an indirect and negative way.
*For one victim which it leads down into
the depths of idiocy, there are scores and
hundreds whom it makes shame-faced,
languid, irresolute and inefficient for any
high purpose of life.* In this way, the
wrong to individuals and to the community is very great. It behooves every parent, especially those whose children (of
either sex) are obliged to board and sleep
with other children, whether in boarding-
schools, boarding-houses or elsewhere, to
have a constant and watchful eye over
them with a view to this insidious and
pernicious habit. The symptoms of it
are easily learned, and if once seen should
be immediately noticed. *Nothing is more*

*false than the common doctrine of delicacy
and reserve in the treatment of this habit.*
All hints, all direct advice, all attempts to
cure it by creating diversions will generally do nothing but increase the cunning
with which it is concealed. The way is to
throw aside all reserve; to charge the
offense directly home; to show up its disgusting nature and hideous consequences
in glowing colors; to apply the cautery
seething hot and press it into the very
quick, unsparingly and unceasingly.

" In some families which are degraded
by drunkenness and vice there is a degree
of combined ignorance and depravity
which disgraces humanity. It is not
wonderful that feeble-minded children are
born in such families; or, being born, become idiotic. Out of this class, domestics
are sometimes taken by those in better
circumstances, and they make their employers feel the consequences of suffering
ignorance and vice. There are cases recorded where servant-women who had
charge of little girls deliberately taught
them habits of self-abuse in order that
they might exhaust themselves and go to
sleep quietly. This has happened in pri-

vate homes as well as in alms-houses, and such little girls have become idiotic! The mind instinctively recoils from giving credit to such atrocious guilt; nevertheless it exists with all its hideous consequences, and no hiding of our eyes or wearing of rose-colored spectacles—nothing but looking at it in its naked deformity—will ever enable men to cure it. There is no *cordon sanitaire* for vice; we cannot put it into quarantine, nor shut it up in a hospital. If we allow its existence in our neighborhood, it will poison the very air which our children breathe."

So much from an unquestionable authority as to the character and extent of the secret vice. Let us now look into some of its causes.

First. Bad companions. Perhaps four-fifths of all those who practice masturbation learned the practice from bad companions—a servant, playmate or schoolmate. One medical author asserts that the secret vice of both sexes is almost universal among the young in Russia, and another is authority for the statement that in some European countries nurses very commonly teach little children self-

abuse in order to quiet them, and the
practice is by no means unknown in
America. In some instances, cultured
persons have been known to teach the
habit to promising youths. In one of our
noted educational centers a few years
ago, the superintendent of the city schools
—a story almost incredible, but nevertheless true—deliberately initiated a number
of his best pupils into the mysteries of
this vice. He was reported to the board
of directors, and for this inhuman act
deservedly lost his position. After one of
my lectures to men only in a western
State, a single man thirty-one years old
came to me and asked advice. He stated
that he did not know what self-abuse
was until he was twenty-eight years old.
Then his bed-fellow one evil night taught
it to him. He practiced it one year without realizing his danger, when he chanced
upon a book which called his attention to
the harmfulness of the habit. He quit at
once, but the evil effects of his year's dissipation followed. The teaching of God's
word that "evil communications corrupt
good manners" is nowhere more true
than here, and as it is almost impossible to

keep a child from knowing more or less of bad company sooner or later in life, the only way to save him is to forewarn.

Second. Exasperating physical conditions. "A constipated condition of the bowels, the irritation of thread worms in the rectum, and, particularly, irritation arising from inattention to local cleanliness, may give rise to the habit by provoking rubbing or scratching of the parts." An abnormal length of the prepuce, or fore-skin, is not an uncommon cause of the early practice of masturbation among boys. Dr. Crutcher asserts that about one-fourth of the boys of the present generation are born this way. The only sensible thing to do in such cases is to have the child circumcised—a simple performance which almost any surgeon understands. If this is not done, the result will be an accumulation of filthy and exasperating secretions within the folds of the prepuce, and few, if any, such victims will escape masturbation. Very often a surgical operation is absolutely necessary upon males, and some females too, in order to remove physical causes of excessive desires for sexual gratification.

Third. Improper food and drink. I sometimes fear that we Americans are fast becoming a nation of gormands. We set the finest tables, I suppose, of any country under the sun. The result is that our nervous system is kept strung up to concert pitch all the time, and it is little wonder that we break so many strings of personal purity. Liquor and tobacco are deadly foes to sexual cleanliness. These poisons should never be used under any circumstances. No child should be allowed to use tea or coffee, and adults should use these stimulants sparingly. All highly seasoned foods should be avoided by amorous natures, for I am morally certain that they constitute a very common cause of self-abuse on the part of the unmarried, and sexual excesses on the part of the married.

Fourth. Unclean thoughts. Many youths, and older men too, who would perhaps scorn to visit a house of ill-fame, or to seduce a pure girl, take delight in picturing to themselves scenes of sexual luxury. In other words, they commit mental adultery and fornication. Many an innocent female is thus made the victim of

an unholy passion. Many promising boys
and talented men are thus led into ruin's
path. The well-known triplet "Sow a
thought, and you reap a deed; sow a deed,
and you reap a character; sow a character,
and you reap a destiny" finds no better
illustration, perhaps, than in the case of
mental sensualists. It is impossible for a
man to keep himself pure who habitually
harbors impure thoughts. The lust thus
stirred up will speedily seek gratification;
and if the individual is too conscientious
to engage in illicit intercourse, he falls
into the fearful habit of self-abuse. In
this manner thousands of bright lives are
blighted forever.

Fifth. Idleness. Satan is always ready
to pay a premium upon idle hands. The
state of having nothing to do is one of the
most dangerous things in the world to
young and old. Every day should be well
spent. The practice of lying abed late in
the morning is a very deplorable one—a
sworn enemy to both physical and mental
purity.

"There is a great difference in boys regarding the formation of these habits,"
says Dr. Guernsey. "While some may

almost insensibly glide into them, others, intuitively, as it were, turn away from all such temptations, and banish all thoughts of a sexual nature from their minds at once. This is right. So long as a boy's mind refuses to harbor such baleful approaches, so long he is safe; but the moment he heeds them and allows them to enter his mind, that moment he is in danger, and will most likely fall into bad habits. He must strenuously resist all such thoughts, and, going to his father or mother, tell them about his trials and temptations, and strive to forget them until success crowns his efforts. By persistent efforts, by repeated prayers to the Lord for help, by reading his Bible and good, pure stories, by running in the open air, and indulging in some useful occupation, or joyous, healthful play, he will eventually conquer them and thus rise to the dignity of a true man. Sometimes too it may be necessary to consult the physician for help. In addition to the instinctive shrinking which every right-minded person feels from putting ideas of impurity into a child's innocent mind, a parent's pride leads him to hope that *his* boy would not indulge in any such mean and disgusting practices. But, bearing in mind the advice of Herbert Spencer that the aim of discipline should be to produce a *self-governing* being, the best advice a parent or guardian can and *ought* to give is this: *Do not harbor bad thoughts or feelings about anything; at once turn them away and think of something else—of something good, pure and true. Indulge in no hatred or revengeful feelings towards others; plot no evil things; always be true to your word, faithful to your duties, and charitable to all.* And further, a child should be *taught* what 'chastity' really is, instead of leaving him to find it out as best he may. It should be clearly explained to him that true chastity requires the shunning of all indecency and foul language: that he should refrain from touching his secret parts except when the necessities of nature require it; that all sexual emotions should be subjugated. When he grows older, ever boy should be taught that *chastity means continence*; and it should be firmly impressed upon his mind that all lascivious actions are a drain upon his whole system and weaken

the powers which the Lord has given him
to be employed *only* in the married state.
These are characteristics of a true man,
and will help him very much to keep out
of sexual difficulties, which are among the
greatest curses of life."

Concerning the symptoms and results of
masturbation, Dr. Kellogg, a great authority on all sexual subjects, says: "It
is of the utmost importance that parents
should be thoroughly conversant with the
evidences by means of which the addic-
tion to this unwholesome vice may be discovered. It should be remarked at the
outset that only detection in the act can
be considered as absolutely positive proof,
and that no single symptom of the
practice should be considered as conclusive evidence, but when a large number of
the signs enumerated are present in a
given case, the evidence may be considered
sufficiently conclusive to warrant the employment of radical measures to reform
the child. The following are among the
leading signs of self-abuse :—

"1. Change in character. If a boy
has been bright, cheerful, obedient, frank
and energetic, and becomes, without any

apparent cause, fretful, irritable, sullen, stupid, and reticent, the evidence is very strong that he has become addicted to this evil practice.

"2. Sudden decline in health without any acute illness or other apparent cause. It should be remembered, however, that intestinal worms, disorders of digestion, loss of sleep, over-study and over-work may produce such an impairment of health as to give rise to loss of flesh, general weakness, paleness of the face, black circles about the eyes, and other symptoms of exhaustion, although these cases of decline are far less frequent than the one first referred to. Sometimes the symptoms of decline are so great that the child or youth is supposed to be suffering from consumption. In such a case a physical examination of the lungs will show no disease, but a thorough investigation will disclose the fact that the individual is a masturbator. It ought to be mentioned, however, that the practice may actually give rise to consumption, so that the disease may really exist when the habit is present, as the result of its long continuance.

"3. Precocious development is another suspicious symptom. A child that has a senile look, needs looking after.

"4. Deficiency of development is likewise a result of the same cause. When practised extensively, it stunts the growth in a most remarkable degree. The chest, instead of expanding, remains flat and narrow. The limbs are lank and feeble. The voice does not acquire its natural depth and fullness. Even the development of the beard at proper age is deficient. Both mind and body suffer from the devitalizing influence of the vice.

"5. Unnatural languor, lassitude and dullness, especially in the morning, should attract attention. A healthy child is naturally active and full of life and animal spirits. The traits named, especially if accompanied by vacancy of expression, may well give rise to suspicion.

"6. Love of being alone is another very suspicious sign which lays the child open to grave suspicion of being addicted to this vice. A child that habitually secretes itself from observation should be carefully watched.

"7. Unnatural timidity in a child that previously had natural self-possession and confidence. There are other causes of timidity, however, and it would certainly be very wrong to accuse every bashful child of being addicted to this practice.

"8. An appearance of unnatural boldness is a not infrequent symptom. Some young men, knowing that inability to look a person in the eye is regarded as a suspicious symptom of the habit, assume an appearance of boldness, which is quite as unnatural as the symptom which he undertakes to hide. We have sometimes been told by persons addicted to this habit that they frequently found themselves staring at people in a most disagreeable way, but seemed to be powerless to help themselves.

"9. A capricious appetite in children, while sometimes the result of dyspepsia or intestinal worms, is very frequently the result of this practice. Tobacco-using should also be mentioned as a suspicious sign. Although it is not directly the result of the practice, it is pretty certain to be accompanied by it. Depraved habits, such as the eating of clay, chalk, slate pencils, etc., are frequently observed in these cases.

"10. Roundness of shoulders or a stooping posture in sitting sometimes results from these causes.

"11. An unnaturally stiff, wriggling gait is sometimes due to the same cause.

"12. Extreme nervousness, twitching of the muscles, and lack of self-control are symptoms seen in children addicted to this practice.

"13. Little boys who show a decided preference for the society of little girls need careful watching.

"14. The boy who complains of pain in the back, weakness of the legs, and headache, if he has previously been a strong and healthy child, is probably addicted to bad habits.

"15. Unnatural size and fullness of the superficial veins of the body, particularly of the hands, feet and legs, are symptoms worthy of attention.

"16. Wetting the bed is frequently the result of an unnatural irritability of the parts, produced by self-abuse.

"17. Palpitation of the heart and irregular beating of the heart are frequently the result of this cause.

"18. In older boys, pimples upon the face, especially when appearing upon the forehead, as well as upon other parts of the face, are strong evidences of irritation of the sexual organs, produced by self-abuse.

"19. Epileptic fits, occurring in young c h i l d r e n who have previously been healthy, should lead to a careful examination of the child's habits.

"20. Constant coldness and moisture of the palms in young persons who are not suffering from any constitutional malady frequently arise from the exhaustion produced by masturbation.

"21. In boys who begin the practice some years before puberty, there is generally an abnormal development of the parts. If the practice is continued some time after puberity, the organs become relaxed and diminished in size.

"22. Stains upon the underclothing, night-clothing or bedding should lead to an investigation.

"Parents should carefully observe the habits of their children, and on discovery of any of the above-named symptoms, should make a thorough-going examination of the matter. Parents are very likely to be easily led to believe that *their* children, at least, are innocent. The fact is, children are very much alike, and a somewhat extensive observation has convinced us that intellectual children—those who have had good moral training, and would seem to be less likely to acquire this evil habit—are even more likely to become addicted to it, than those of a lower grade of intellect who have more robust bodies, and hence a healthier condition of the nervous system. The first class, in consequence of a more highly sensitive organism, are more excitable and more easily fascinated by the destroying vice.

"The body never attains full development when this habit is begun at an early age and indulged after sexual development. All the vital powers are weakened. Undoubtedly the indulgence of this vile practice affords an ample explanation for the great number of puny, scrawny, weak-backed, lank-limbed, hollow-eyed, pale, sallow-faced boys who may always be seen upon the streets of any city. *But a small proportion of the young men of the present day possess one-half the vitality and stamina which properly belong to their age of life. Their vitality has been wasted and sapped by this monster of vice which has become so well nigh universal among the youth of civilized lands.* Weakness of the back, feebleness of the muscles, loss of appetite, slow digestion or dyspepsia, nervousness, impairment of vision, loss of energy—these are but a few of the physical consequences of this horrible practice. Long and frequent indulgence of this disgusting habit often brings on a general decline. The patient loses flesh, grows pale and weak, begins to cough, and almost before he is aware that danger is threatened, finds himself a victim of that hopeless malady, consumption."

Eminent authorities say that *one drop of semen,* that life fluid which makes a man a man, is *worth twenty drops of the purest blood.* No wonder then that its ruthless waste is damaging in the extreme. Suppose that you would tap an artery and extract therefrom one hundred drops of blood, two, five or ten times a week, what

would be the result? No worse than to
practice this body and soul-destroying
habit of self-abuse two, five or ten times a
week as thousands of suffering youths are
doing to-day. Hippocrates said that "the
seed of man arises from all the humors of
the body, and is the most valuable part of
them." And another authority remarks
that "the semen is kept in the seed ves-
sels until the man makes proper use of it
or *nocturnal emissions deprive him of it.*
During all this time the quantity which is
there detained excites him to the act of
venery; but the greater part of this essence,
which is the most volatile and odoriferous,
as well as the strongest, is absorbed into
the blood, and it there produces, upon
its return, very great changes. It makes
the beard, hair and nails grow; it changes
the voice and manners—for age does not
produce these changes in animals; it is
the seed only that operates in this manner,
for these changes are never met with in
eunuchs, or those who have been deprived
of their testicles. Can a greater proof of
its vitalizing power be shown than the
fact that one single drop is sufficient,
under proper circumstances, to give life to

a future being?" What a deplorable thing
it is, therefore, to lose by passion or disease this important element.

Many boys imagine that they can't be
men until they prove themselves able to
expend semen. Others again believe that
nature requires an occasional unloading of
the accumulation of this vital article; but
the idea is absurd. Some physicians, 'tis
true, be it said to their everlasting disgrace, have taught this hurtful theory.
But the ablest physiologists are agreed in
the fact that no such expenditure is
necessary. "Man in a healthy state,"
asserts Dr. Guernsey, *"need not and
should not lose one drop of seminal fluid
by his own hand, by nightly emissions or
pollutions, or in any way,* until he becomes
conjoined to a wife of his choice in the holy
bonds of matrimony. Every time the
seed of his body is lost in a disorderly or
unnatural way, he injures the finest
textures of his brain correspondingly, as
well as the finest and most excellent condition of his mind and soul, because the
act proceeds in its incipiency from a willful
prostitution of these higher powers."

Self-abuse is a deadly enemy to memory.

It induces fickleness of mind, irritability, strangeness of manner, and crankiness. It brings on epilepsy, heart disease, lung trouble, impotency, and a multitude of diseases and infirmities in different cases. In short, self-abuse blunts the manhood of man and the womanhood of woman as no other evil under the sun can do. I sometimes feel like denouncing masturbation as the living incarnation of all that's hellish, for it seems that the practice of this foul habit can do all to unman man that all other habits can do and much more.

It is a very common cause of insanity. In this all authorities are agreed. When delivering my lecture to men only at Chariton, Iowa, in August, 1891, I was interrupted by Mr. O. E. Payne, a member of the County Board of Examiners on cases of insanity. He apologized for rising in the midst of the address, but said that he wished to indorse all I had said concerning the injuriousness of self-abuse upon the mental faculties. He asserted that his board had found the practice of this habit to be one of the most prolific causes of insanity in the subjeots presented for their consideration. Esquiral says: " Masturbation, that torment of the human species, is more often than one thinks the cause of insanity, especially in the houses of the rich." And Dr. Arnold declares that "authors are universally agreed, from Galen down to the present day, concerning the pernicious influence of this enervating indulgence and its strong propensity to generate the very worst and most formidable kinds of insanity. It has frequently been known to occasion speedy and even instant insanity."

But of all the dire results following the practice of self-abuse, perhaps the most common and at the same time most alarming is that of *spermatorrhœa*. This result follows a few months' or a few years' practice of the habit. Many young men upon reading a work or hearing a lecture on the subject of self-abuse, and in this way learning for the first time of its exceeding sinfulness, quit; but to their utter chagrin and alarm *involuntary emissions* follow. They awake from an amorous dream at night only to find their life-fluid ebbing away. In the society of females, they sometimes suffer from the most unhallowed desires, which, not being gratified, result in thin, mucus-like discharges from the penis, causing an after weakness and debility most distressing. An accidental friction of the clothes or a horse-back ride sometimes causes violent erections, which are also followed by exhaustion and a feeling of prostration. If he ventures upon matrimonial life, such a sufferer will find that the pleasure of copulation is greatly marred, both for himself and his companion, by his inability to satisfactorily complete the act—a premature emission of semen reminding him all too forcibly of the secret sins of youth. "After frequent nocturnal emissions," says Hoffman, "not only the powers are lost, the body falls away, and the face turns pale, but, moreover, the memory fails. A cold sensation seizes all the limbs, the sight is cloudy, and the voice becomes hoarse. All the body languishes by degrees. Distracting dreams prevent sleep administering any relief, and such pains ensue as are felt from the blows of a cudgel."

In advanced stages of spermatorrhœa,

the victim sustains several emissions a week, and, in some cases, several every twenty-four hours. In such instances, speedy relief must be obtained or a coffin, one or the other. It is possible for some strong constitutions to endure quite a heavy drain for years. Others will give away in as many months under the same pressure. But in any case, involuntary emissions are dangerous. Dr. Parker declares that "nocturnal emissions occurring more frequently than once in fourteen nights are decided signs of debility and certain harbingers of approaching impotence." Some authors assert that frequent nocturnal emissions are speedily followed by diurnal losses. When passing urine, the patient also passes, unconsciously, a quantity of semen. And upon the slightest sensual provocation, such as a glance at an impure picture, the reading of a too-suggestive paragraph in book or paper, or a momentary contact with women in social intercourse, an involuntary dribbling occurs, which causes not only a feeling of great weariness and remorse, but, if the sufferer is not very attentive to cleanliness, an unpleasant smell. In the worst cases, the erectile power of the victim becomes prostrate, and he becomes loathsome to himself and everybody else, especially to her who calls him husband, if he is so unfortunate as to enter himself in the married state in this condition. "In losing before the usual age the generative functions," says Lallemand, "man loses the consciousness of his dignity, because he feels himself fallen in importance in relation to his species. In consequence, the loss of virile power produces an effect more overpowering than that of honors, fortune, friends, or relations; even the loss of liberty is as nothing as compared to this internal and continual torture."

Oh, the suffering and sorrow brought on by self-abuse! I trust that these lines may be carefully perused by thousands of youths who have as yet not polluted themselves, and who, from these frightful but truthful pictures of this hideous evil, will resolve to keep themselves forever clean in thought, word, and act.

"But is there any hope for those who are already suffering from the result of self-pollution?" says one. "Can sperma-torrhœa be cured?"

I answer unhesitatingly, yes. At least in nine cases out of ten, and the tenth will probably never read this book. For *you*, therefore, there is hope.

"Well, what shall I take? With whom shall I doctor?"

There it is, *take, take, take.* This is the prevalent notion, that the only way to cure one's self is to take something—gulp down at stated intervals a few gallons of sickening drugs. And in this way medical quacks and charlatans get in their work to the financial and physical detriment of the deluded. In some aggravated cases, a little medicine is necessary, and in such instances my advice would be, consult your family physician. Keep nothing back, but unfold your shame to him fully. He will probably be able to give you relief. If not, he can take you to some trustworthy specialist who can. But do not spend one cent for the concoctions advertised so extensively by sharpers who "guarantee" to cure you within a certain number of days, etc. Their letters, pamphlets, and question lists often do incalculable damage in scaring the sufferer, as well as in fleecing him of his ducats. Medicines can only palliate in this ailment. The great and imperative thing is to *remove the causes* and *keep them removed.* Then the patient can cure himself. Involuntary emissions are dangerous, and a sufferer, therefore, should lose no time in stopping them; but getting scared over the matter will not aid in effecting a cure by any means. I am convinced that a steady mind and persevering will are the most powerful agents in the treatment of spermatorrhœa as in all other diseases.

In this connection allow me to quote a few paragraphs from the gifted pen of Dr. Dio Lewis:

"One of the obstacles to cure in this common and afflicting malady," says this distinguished author, "is the notion that the disease may be gotten rid of by opening the mouth and swallowing medicine. The patient cannot understand you when you assure him that *he must cure himself.* This, of course, is true of many or of most disorders, but especially so of the ailment under consideration.   Permit me to mention a case with some of its details:

"An intelligent young man of twenty-four, a victim of nocturnal emissions, came to consult me.   He told me a sad story, in which at least six advertising medical sharks figured.   He had paid them in all about $400, had taken many nauseous and injurious drugs, had been greatly annoyed with the wearing of rings and other absurd machines, and, of course, was no better—on the contrary very much worse.   But, notwithstanding all this bitter experience, he was greatly surprised and disappointed when I told him that a physician could do nothing for him —that he must *cure himself!*

"'But, Doctor, what shall I take? what? what?   How am I to get well if I do not take something?'

"I found it up-hill business to explain the utter worthlessness of drugs in such a case.   Having at last secured his attention, I said: Now, I will tell you how to cure yourself.

PRESCRIPTION FOR ONE TROUBLED WITH EITHER SPERMATORRHŒA OR WITH SEXUAL LONGINGS.

"1. Eat very plain but nutritious food, in moderate quantities, for breakfast and for dinner Go without supper. (Beef, mutton, b.ead made of unbolted flour, oatmeal, potatoes, cracked. wheat, and fruit are proper articles. But do not disturb your digestion with fruits or anything else between meals, and beware of taking too much animal food. Avoid spirits and malt liquors, coffee, tea, tobacco, oysters, rich fish, pork, all fat and salted meats, pastry, sweetmeats, and stimulating condiments. Don't keep vexing your mind about this and that kind of food, but settle down promptly and decidedly on what medical men have ascertained to be the best, and don't be forever questioning if you can't squeeze in a little of this or a bit of that.)

"2. Drink nothing but pure, soft water; of that as freely as you like on going to bed and on getting up in the morning.

"3. Retire early; rise early. Sleep in a well-ventilated room. Avoid a soft bed, and particularly soft pillows.

"4. Rub yourself all over with hair gloves on going to bed. When you rise, moisten your skin all over with cold water, and follow with coarse towels. (Be careful to remove with soap and water every particle of secretion from under the foreskin.)

"5. Work hard at something. If possible, get yourself thoroughly fatigued every day. (Idleness is the mother of concupiscence.)

"6. Keep your feet and legs thoroughly warm.

"7. Cleanse your mind from all impure fancies. Stop at once and forever all lascivious thought. You can do so if you are only resolute. Steer clear of all dalliance, of all love-plays, and love-stories generally.

"8. Cultivate the acquaintance and society of refined, intelligent, and noble women—of your mother and sisters, and of some pure-minded girl who may possibly one day become your wife.

"9. Cultivate also the consciousness, 'Thou God seest me;' the prayerful temper, and a desire to become a fit abode for the indwelling Spirit. Temperance, hard work, abundant sleep, cleanliness, ennobling companionship, and an earnest desire for purity, *persevered in*, will restore your health, spirits, and self-respect.

"Where one person is injured by sexual commerce, many are made feverish and nervous by harboring lewd thoughts. Rioting in visions of nude women may exhaust one as much as an excess in actual intercourse. There are multitudes who would never spend a night with an abandoned female, but who rarely meet a young girl without busying their imaginations with her person. This species of indulgence is well-nigh universal; and as it is the source of all other forms—the fountain from which the external vices spring, the nursery of masturbation and excessive coitus—I am surprised to find how little has been said about it. All overt sins and crimes begin, we know, in the thoughts or imagination. A young man allows himself to conjure up visions of naked females. These become habitual and haunt him, until at last the sexual passion absorbs not only his waking thoughts, but his very dreams. Now, if

his education and his surroundings makes
actual intercourse impracticable, he will
probably fall into masturbation; or, if
forewarned in regard to this destructive
practice, he may restrain himself from all
outward indulgence while he still riots in
lascivious fancies. Ah! I wish I could
say what ought to be said in this connection. Here is one of the great fountains
of our woes. Although we may outwardly present a blameless life, how many
of us could wear a window in our breasts
without covering our faces for shame?

"So far as the record is preserved, unchastity has contributed above all other
causes to the exhaustion and demoralization of the race. And we shall not be
likely to vanquish this monster, even in
ourselves, unless we make *the thoughts*
our point of attack. So long as *they* are
libidinous, we are indulging in sexual
abuse, and we are almost sure, when
temptation comes, to commit the overt
acts of sin. If we cannot succeed within,
we may pray in vain for help to resist the
tempter outwardly. But if we ask for assistance to *cleanse the inner man*, and
supplement our prayers by hearty effort,

we are sure to win. A sincere, earnest
determination in this direction will never
fail."

"When sexual thoughts and temptations arise in one's mind," says good Dr.
Guernsey, "even very young men are
capable of putting them away, urged by
the thought that tampering with one's
generative organs is wrong. He should
intuitively feel that it is something akin
to theft, or a crime of some worse sort, for
him to indulge in solitary vice—he should
intuitively feel an inward reproach for all
such meditations. When one is sorely
tempted in these matters, as is often the
case, let him reflect that he was not
created to indulge in such pleasures by
himself, and that to do so is a crime—a
sin against the God of heaven; that it is
his destiny, his privilege, and one of the
uses of his life to share such enjoyments
with the wife of his bosom; and that all excitement or dallying with this part of his
nature before marriage, only serves to
weaken his sexual powers, as well as his
mind and body. Also that it mars his sexual uses, and will detract from his sexual
pleasures in the married life. Sexual in-

dulgence of any sort in a young man is a loss, not only to himself, but also, prospectively, to that dear girl whom he will some day make his wife. Such reflections will often drive away temptation entirely. If they are not sufficient to do so, let him read some interesting book that shall take his mind away from the subject, or, that failing, let him take exercise—*vigorous* exercise, pushed to fatigue if necessary. If these states of temptation occur in bed at night, let him rise and read, plunge his arm into very cold water, or go forth into the open air and seek relief in a rapid walk. It is better to go to any amount of trouble, and to endure any physical discomfort, than to sacrifice one's chastity, the loss of which can never be replaced.

"A young man naturally desires and expects chastity of the strictest order in the young woman of his choice for a wife. Who would marry a girl, no matter how beautiful or how many and varied her accomplishments, if it were known that she had granted her favors to any other man? And yet what less has *she* a perfect right to require the strictest purity from a young man who presumes to pay his ad-

dresses to her? This consideration, too,
should serve as a restraint to any amorous
desires that might infest a man's mind. It
is wonderful how keen are the perceptions
of a pure-minded young lady to detect
even an approach to licentiousness in the
male. He is abhorrent to her, and his very
sphere betrays him."

In addition to the foregoing powerful
agencies in effecting a cure for unhallowed
desires, self-abuse and involuntary emissions, I would recommend an occasional
hot water injection into the rectum. Let
the patient fill a large bowl with water
just as warm as he can bear it. Use
enough of the best toilet soap to make a
light suds. Then take a common bulb
syringe, and force as much of the water
into the colon as he can possibly hold. It
will be quite difficult at first, but in a few
weeks he will find himself able to take up
from two to four quarts. Retain it a few
minutes, meanwhile gently kneading the
abdomen, and then let it all pass.
This process is known as "flushing the
colon," and is highly recommended by
Dr. A. Wilford Hall, of New York, and
others, as a cure for constipation, bilious-

ness, and all diseases arising from a clogged condition of the digestive machinery. After the rectum is thoroughly cleansed in this manner, proceed to take another injection of about one quart. Retain this over night. Always take these injections the last thing before retiring—never closely following a meal. There will be some difficulty at first in retaining the water over night; but it can be done, as the experience of thousands has demonstrated. Surprising as it may seem to the reader, the water thus retained will pass through the system in such a manner as to thoroughly cleanse the kidneys and organs of procreation. The effect will be most helpful to the patient in many ways. Dr. Hall published a pamphlet fully explaining this medicineless, expenseless, but truly hygienic treatment, and I would that every sufferer from sexual disorders in the world might possess a copy of it and put its excellent suggestions into practice. Twice a week is often enough to use this treatment.

Another good expedient is the thorough bathing of the secret parts in cold water just before retiring. This not only ena-

bles the patient to keep these organs scru-
pulously clean, but it drives the hot blood
away from them, and helps to cool his all-
too-ardent passion.

In some cases a little medicine may be
used by way of palliation. I will therefore give a few prescriptions. It may
prove a blessing to those who from excessive timidity or other reasons would not
consult a reputable physician. But as a
rule, if it seems absolutely necessary to
call in the assistance of drugs, I would
advise every sufferer to consult his family
physician.

Dr. Kellogg, in his "Man the Master-
piece," page 586, gives the following *Prescriptions for Sexual Nervous Debility:*

I.

R.   Sodæ Brom............dr. 4.
     Ammon, Brom.........dr. 4.
     Aquæ ....oz. 3.

Dose: Take in water one teaspoonful
at night on going to bed.

II.

R.   Atropia Sulp...........gr. ¼
     Aquæ................ ....oz. 4

Dose: Teaspoonful at night.

"Those two remedies are very useful in cases where the nocturnal losses occur with great frequency, and are not readily controlled by the simple means elsewhere recommended. They are the only drugs which we consider of any value whatever in the treatment of these maladies. They must not be depended upon for effecting a cure, however. They only palliate and give temporary relief from one of the most annoying systems."

Dr. Chase, in his last "Receipt Book," gives the following *Tonic Tincture for Impotency, Spermatorrhœa, etc.:*

"Dr. R. M. Griswold, of North Manchester, Conn., reports through the *Brief* that he has made several quick cures of the above diseases, with the following tinctures of nux vomica and cantharides, each 1 dr.; tincture ferri-mur (muriated tincture of iron) 3 drs.; fl. ex. ergot, 1 oz. acidi phos. dil. (dilute phosphoric acid), 3 drs.; mix. [The author would say, double the amount, as it will be needed.] Dose: Thirty drops (one-half teaspoonful) in a wine-glass of water three times daily. 'Within the last six months,' the Doctor says, 'I have treated several cases of the

above diseases with uniform success, a
radical cure being effected in each case.
Two cases occurred in young men of about
twenty years of age, resulting from masturbation; one case following gonorrhea;
the fourth case, a married man, was the
result of excessive indulgence; and in
three other cases, where the search for the
direct cause was unsuccessful—yet the
same treatment succeeded.' He required
abstinence from all stimulants (liquors)
and condiments (highly seasoned food),
using light but nourishing food, especially
milk, eggs, fish; sleeping on a hard bed,
and in a cold, well-ventilated room; total
avoidance of all sexual excitement, and all
undue exertion of strength. By observing
the foregoing the success was satisfactory."

Dr. Chase also endorses the following
prescription, recommended by Dr. Geo.
W. Homsher, of Fairfield, Iowa:

"Ferro cyanuret of potash, one-half oz.;
aq.bul.(boiling water) three ozs.; dissolve;
then add glycerine, one and one-half ozs.;
specific tincture of staphisagria, one dr.
Dose: One teaspoonful three times daily,
and at bed-time the patient should take a

sponge bath over the spine and hips, and, on retiring, ften grains of lupulin." Dr. Homsher declared that this treatment would not only relieve the discharge of semen, but cure nine cases out of ten of sexual debility, if the patient would take the medicines faithfully, and abstain from sexual intercourse for at least two months.

Dr. R. W. McCandlass, of Emporia, Kansas, also recommends lupulin in doses of from ten to thirty grains, taken at bed-time, as a preventive of nocturnal emissions.

But none of these excellent remedies, or all of them put together, will effect a cure unless the patient endeavors to cure himself by observing the rules previously given on inward and outward chastity. Herein lies the root of the whole matter. All baneful causes must be removed before satisfactory effects can possibly obtain.

Right here let me warn you against visiting a woman with the fond hope of curing involuntary emissions. Some physicians advise this course, be it said to their everlasting shame. If one should ever give you such pernicious advice, just say to him: " Very well, Doctor, bring in

your wife or daughter," and see how
quickly he will fly into a rage. Oh, no!
his wife and daughter are too pure and
holy for such shameful usage. Well, how
much more precious to him are his loved
ones than those of any other man? Every
woman, fallen or unfallen, is *some man's*
wife or daughter, and the physician who
would give such advice deserves to be
kicked out of town. Aside from all moral
reasons such advice is folly, for the ablest
writers are agreed in the fact that intercourse under such circumstances can but
palliate symptoms at best, and cannot cure.
"Two wrongs can never make a right."

And now in concluding this chapter, I
want to urge the necessity of good hard
work, mental or physical, or both. Dr.
Watts was right when he sang—

> "For satan finds some mischief still
> For idle hands to do."

Earnest toil, incessant toil, tremendous
toil, is necessary to make a man what he
ought to be in this busy world. This active age has little use for the lazy man or
the man who pretends that he wants to
work but cannot find anything to do.
No; something is demanded of every man

who would share in the world's prosperity,
and there is plenty to do. Says Owen
Meredith:

> "God be thanked that the dead have left still
> Good undone for the living to do—
> Still some aim for the heart and the will
> And the soul of a man to pursue."
>
> —*Epilogue.*

Then work. Do something. When lust
begins knocking at your door, arise and
set about some honorable task. Busy the
mind and busy the hands. With lofty
impulse pursue duty, and half the battle
against unchastity is won.

"Understand always," says Thomas
Carlyle, "that the end of man is an action,
not a thought. Endeavor incessantly
with all the strength that is in you to
ascertain what you can do in this world,
and upon that bend your whole faculties,
regarding all reveries, feelings, singular
thoughts, and moods, as worth nothing
whatever except as they bear on that and
will help you toward that. Your thoughts,
moods, etc., will thus in part legitimate
themselves and become fruitful possessions for you. No one ever understood
this universe, but each one may understand what good and manful work it is

possible to accomplish here. All true
work is sacred; in all true work, be it but
true hand-labour, there is something of
divineness. Blessed is he who has found
his work; let him ask no other blessedness.
He has a work, a life purpose; he has
found it and will follow it."

If you are so fortunate as to hold fellow-
ship with Christ and His church, supplement all your own efforts with prayer.
Steep your every undertaking in the spirit
of humble, trustful, expectant petition to
God. Have you made many mistakes in
the past? Have you fallen from truth,
purity and peace? Then *turn about*, FACE,
NOW! There is hope for you. Rise to
your true manhood. Let by-gones be
by-gones; but in the future, make your
record clean. You can do it. You may
fail at first in the attempt to do so, but
try again. Persevere. Victory will not
be long in crowning your honest efforts.
Let the language of the great apostle to
the Gentiles, "I can do all things through
Christ who strengtheneth me," be your
watch-cry. So shall you be triumphant!

May the Lord bless this chapter in the
salvation from the secret vice, or the un-

natural sin of masturbation, of thousands who are now suffering therefrom, whether knowingly or ignorantly, is my devout wish.

CHAPTER IX.

PRIVATE WORDS TO YOUNG MEN.

You are here. Did you ever stop and ask of your higher consciousness, What am I here for? If not, I beg of you, young man, to lose no time in doing so.

Many young men—ah! yes, the vast majority of them—live as if there were no hereafter, and consequently as if the thing to do were to have a jolly good time while opportunity presents itself. The motto of this class seems to be " eat, drink and be merry, for to-morrow we die." Hence they plunge full length into all forms of dissipation, and by middle-age reap diseased bodies, weakened minds, scanty purses and blighted honor.

How deplorable that a young man should waste his youth! All authors are agreed in denominating youth the golden period of life. "Augustine calls youth '*flos ætatis*,' —the flower of our days; Cicero calls it '*bona ætas*'—the blessed time, and Seneca, '*ætas optima*'—the best of life. The Elizabethan writers often speak of 'the primrose of our youth.'" The best prose and poetry of all literature describes youth with the choicest figures of speech.

Youth should be well spent, for once gone it is gone forever. "Some things God gives often," says Geike; "some He gives only once. The seasons return again and again, and the flowers change with the month; but youth comes twice to none. While we have it we think little of it, but we never cease to look back to it fondly when it is gone." La Rochefoucauld says: "Youth is a continual intoxication; it is the fever of reason." And an ancient Roman authority declares that "it is a truth but too well known that rashness attends youth, as prudence does old age."

But why should it be so? God has not placed you here, my dear young friend, to spend your days in idleness and dissipation. He has not placed you here to live for self alone. It was never the purpose

of our Divine Creator that you should
prostitute your time, talents and opportunities to the service of the world, the
flesh, and the devil. You are here for a
good purpose, and the sooner you are
brought to realize this fact and govern
yourself accordingly, the better.

Don't sow any wild oats. It used to be
considered a matter of course that young
men should sow a nice little piece of their
earlier life with wild oats, and this foolish
and hurtful idea is quite prevalent in some
circles yet. I don't know where this idea
originated ;certainly not in any good man's
heart. But it's in the air, and multitudes
are being injured by it.   I am glad, however, to observe a growing disposition on
the part of the better elements of society
everywhere to discountenance youthful indiscretions. "It seems to be more generally recognized," says a modern writer,
" that if young persons poison their bodies
and corrupt their minds with vicious
courses, no lapse of time after a reform is
likely to restore them to physical soundness and the soul-purity of their earlier
days."

Mr. Hughes, the noted author of " Tom

Brown at Oxford," gives us the following
pregnant paragraph on the subject before
us:

"In all the wide range of accepted
British maxims there is none, take it all
in all, more thoroughly abominable than
this one as to the sowing of wild oats.
Look at it on what side you will, and I
defy you to make anything but a devil's
maxim out of it. What a man, be he
young, old or middle-aged, sows, *that* and
nothing else shall he reap. The only
thing to do with wild oats is to put them
carefully into the hottest part of the fire
and get them burnt to dust, every seed of
them. If you sow them, no matter in
what ground, up they will come with long
tough roots and luxuriant stalks and
leaves, as sure as there is a sun in heaven.
The devil too, whose special crop they
are, will see that they thrive, and you,
and nobody else, will have to reap them;
and no common reaping will get them out
of the soil, which must be dug deep, again
and again. Well for you if with all your
care, you can make the ground sweet
again by your dying day."

A greater than Mr. Hughes says: "Be

not deceived; God is not mocked: for whatsoever a man soweth, that shall he also reap." (Gal. 6:7.)

Beware of bad habits; form good ones, and keep yourself continually under their developing power. " The whole character may be said to be comprehended in the term *habits*," says Rev. John Todd in his celebrated "Students Manual;" "so that it is not far from being true that 'man' is a bundle of habits.' Suppose you were compelled to wear an iron collar about your neck through life, or a chain upon your ankle, would it not be a burden every day and hour of your existence? You rise in the morning a prisoner to your chain; you lie down at night weary with the burden; and you groan the more deeply as you reflect that there is no shaking it off. But even this would be no more intolerable to bear than many of the habits of men; nor would it be more difficult to be shaken off. Habits are easily formed— especially such as are bad; and what to-day seems to be a small affair will soon become fixed and hold you with the strength of a cable. That same cable, you will recollect, is formed by spinning

and twisting one thread at a time, but when once completed, the proudest ship turns her head toward it, and acknowledges her subjection to its power. * *
Do not fear to undertake to form *any* habit which is desirable; for it *can* be formed, and that with more ease than you may at first suppose. *Let the same thing or the same duty return at the same time every day, and it will soon become pleasant.* No matter if it be irksome at first; only let it return periodically every day, and that without any interruption for a time, and it will become a positive pleasure. In this way all our habits are formed."

I want every young man who reads these lines to make a success of life. Want you to be healthy, useful and happy. Permit me therefore to enumerate a few suggestions which I am sure you will find wholesome if you give them a faithful trial.

1. *Have a plan.* Don't allow yourself to float down the stream of life a mere chunk of driftwood. Don't be content to let the *fates* toss you whatever lot they may. But carefully and conscientiously mark out a course and pursue it. Al-

ways endeavor to know one day what you
are going to do the next. Keep your eyes
firmly set on a noble future, and make
straight for the mark. A young man who
carefully plans his life-work, and determinedly adheres to the same in at least
the main, will accomplish five times as
much by the time he is fifty as the young
man who lets circumstances lead him
about by the ears. It is poor policy to
"wait for something to turn up." Go to
work and turn it up yourself. Napoleon
was once asked if he would make a certain move if opportunity presented itself.
"Opportunity!" said the great warrior,
"I *make* opportunities."

2. *Be thoroughly industrious and attentive to details.* God has no use for a lazy
man; satan has. One of the most de-
testable things to see in a young man is
slothfulness. The world demands, and
has a perfect right to do so, habits of industry from every young man who would
share in its advancement. The modern
dude is an excrescence, and deserves the
pity if not the contempt of all right-
thinking people. Every young man should
have an earnest ambition to *be somebody*

and to *do something* worthy in his day.
Industry has accomplished wonders, and
always will. Sigh not for genius, but go
to work. A pound of genuine industry is
usually worth a ton of genius so-called.
"Should you be so unfortunate as to suppose you are a genius, and that things will
come to you, it would be well to undeceive
yourselves as soon as possible," says a
thoughtful writer. "Make up your mind
that industry must be the price of all you
obtain, and at once begin to pay down."
Don't be afraid to do little things lest it
might compromise your dignity! "Diligence in employments of less consequence
is the most successful introduction to
greater enterprises." "We are astonished
at the volumes which the men of former
ages used to write," says Todd. "But the
term *industry* is the key to the whole secret. Demosthenes, as is well known,
copied Thucydides' History eight times
with his own hand, merely to make himself
familiar with the style of that great man.
It was a matter of astonishment to Europe
that Luther, amid all his travels and
active labors, could present a very perfect
translation of the whole Bible. But a

single word explains it all—he had a rigid system of doing something every day. I have never known a man whose habits of everyday industry were so good as those of Jeremiah Evarts. During years of close observation in the bosom of his family, I never saw a day pass without his accomplishing more than he expected. And so regular was he in all his habits that I knew to a moment when I should find him with his pen, and when with his tooth-brush in his hand; and so methodical and thorough, that, though his papers filled many shelves when closely tied up, there was not a paper among all his letters, correspondence, editorial matter, and the like, which was not labeled and in its place, and upon which he could not lay his hand in a moment. I never knew him to search for a paper; it was always in its place. I have never yet met with the man whose industry was so great or who would accomplish so much in a given time. There are two proverbs, one among the Turks, and the other among the Spaniards, both of which contain much that is true. 'A busy man is troubled with but one devil, but the idle man with a thousand.' 'Men are usually tempted by the devil, but the idle man positively tempts the devil!' How much corrupting company, how many temptations to do wrong, how many seasons of danger to your character, and danger to the peace of your friends you would escape by forming the habit of being decidedly industrious every day!" "He that shall walk with vigor three hours a day will pass in seven years a space equal to the circumference of the globe."

"All successful men are agreed in one thing," says Emerson. "They believed that things went not by luck, but by law; that there was not a weak or a cracked link in the chain that joins the first and last of things." And another pertinently says, "Ten thousand trifles attended to— ten thousand orders given and disappointments borne—go to the making up of a triumph." "Diligence," says Franklin, "is the mother of good luck, and God gives all things to industry."

3. *Persevere.* Form the habit of sticking to a task until it is completed. Do nothing by halves. "What is worth doing is worth doing well." In nearly all

great undertakings of your life there will
probably come a time when you will feel
like giving up. But persevere. "To the
victor belongs the spoil." It may require years of arduous toil to bring the
victory; but it will come. The power of
perseverance has been illustrated in the
lives of so many great and successful men
that it would almost seem trite for one to
write at length on the subject. And yet
in this feverish, restless age the lack of
the persistent, tenacious spirit is a very
common fault with young men. They
try one thing a while, and if success does
not immediately crown their efforts, give
it up and try something else. Thus it is
no uncommon thing to see a man who at
forty has dabbled in perhaps twenty different lines of business and failed in all.
Such a course can never result in a Henry
Clay, Lord Beaconsfield, or U. S. Grant.
The bull-dog tenacity of these great
characters, and many others like them, is
well known to students of biography.
This is an age of specialties. The young
man who would succeed in life must
adopt the motto of Paul, "This one thing

I do," and stick to it until a triumphant issue is scored.

Speaking of Gen. Grant as he appeared at Galena in 1860, Gen. Badeau, in a *Century* article, says: " No restless ambition disturbed his spirit. No craving for fame made him dissatisfied with obscurity. Those nearest him never suspected that he possessed extraordinary ability. He himself never dreamed that he was destined for great place or power. Yet his vicissitudes had given him a wide and practical experience, and made him, unknown to himself, a representative American. He had learned patience when hope was long deferred, and endurance under heavy and repeated difficulties; he had displayed audacity in emergencies, as well as persistency of resolve and fertility of resource. If one means failed, he tried another. He was not discouraged by ill fortune, nor discontented with little things. Above all, he never quailed, and never despaired. The leather merchant of Galena was not without preparation even for that great future which awaited him all unknown. There were many traits in him like those of Moltke. Both lived simply and almost unknown to their countrymen for many years. Moltke, it is true, remained in his profession, and was more fortunate as the world goes; but until the great opportunity came, he also was comparatively obscure."

Persistence means victory. So faint not, my brother. Has your life thus far been checkered with disappointments? Does the future appear dark? Despair not, but press on with determined will. By persistent effort you can free yourself of bad habits if a victim of the same, and form better ones. By persistent effort you can turn defeat into triumph.

> "Through efforts long in vain, prophetic need
>   Begets the deed:
> Nerve then thy soul with direst need to cope.
>   Life's brightest hope
> Lies latent in Fate's deadliest lair—
>   Never despair."

4. *Be punctual in all things.* In this magnificent trait nearly every young man of the present generation fails. It is difficult to find an individual to-day concerning whom it may be truly said, "He is the very soul of punctuality." There is no over-production along this line. "We are all so indolent by nature and

by habit," says Todd, "that we feel it a luxury to find a man of real, undeviating punctuality. We love to lean upon such a man, and we are willing to purchase such a staff at almost any price. It shows, at least, that he has conquered himself."

Lord Brougham was noted for his punctuality. While lord chancellor of England, he "presided in the house of lords and in the court of chancery; gave audience daily to the barristers; found time to write reviews; and to be at the head of *ten* associations which were publishing works of useful knowledge." But, busy as he was, and burdened with arduous cares, he was uniformly found in his chair when the hour for business arrived. His strict punctuality enabled him to accomplish wonders. Blackstone also was richly endowed with this virtue. It is said that when delivering his celebrated lectures he was never known to keep his audience waiting a minute. Quite different from many present-day speakers.

Be punctual in the payment of every debt, even if you have to borrow money to pay for borrowed money. Be punctual in keeping every engagement. Don't go

ahead of time; don't go a moment behind
time; but go *on time*. Be punctual at
school, at church, at the office, and everywhere. Don't go through the world half
asleep, apparently taking little interest in
anything and half doing what little you
do attempt. But be wide-awake! Nothing will commend a young man more to
the confidence of the business world than
the habit of undeviating punctuality in
all things, coupled with strict attentive-
ness and thoroughness. I shall never forget a motto learned when a boy from a
successful educator, Prof. John W.
Stewart, of Iowa: "Attention, prompt-
ness, and thoroughness are the essential
elements of success."

5. *Form the habit of early rising.* Late
rising is one of the prominent faults of
this generation. There are various causes
for it, some of them perhaps reasonable
in certain instances. But whatever the
cause, the effect of habitual late rising is
deplorable. "Few ever lived to a great
age, and fewer still ever became distinguished, who were not in the habit of
early rising." Night is the time to sleep
and day the time to work. This is na-

ture's law, and woe be unto him who dis-
regards it. "He who rises late," says
Franklin, "may trot all day and not have
overtaken his business at night." Dean
Swift says somewhere that he "never
knew a man come to greatness and emi-
nence who lay in bed of a morning." It
has been truly, if not very poetically, said
that—

"The early bird catches the worm."

And who has not learned by heart, if he
has failed to put in practice, the familiar
couplet—

"Early to bed and early to rise,
Makes a man healthy, wealthy and wise."

It is practically out of the question, of
course, for one to rise early unless he re-
tires early, for few people can get along
well without seven or eight hours' sleep.
Late hours are damaging to the health
and purity of anybody, generally speaking,
and it would be a blessing to this sin-
cursed world if a reformation could be in-
augurated which would put the race in
bed not later than ten o'clock the year
round. "In the fourteenth century, the
shops in Paris were universally open at

four in the morning; now, not till long
after seven. Then, the king of France
dined out at eight o'clock in the morning
and retired to his chamber at the same
hour in the evening. In the time of
Henry VIII, seven in the morning was
the fashionable breakfast hour—ten the
dinner hour. In the time of Elizabeth,
the nobility, fashionables, and students,
dined at eleven o'clock, and supped between five and six in the afternoon.
Frederick II, of Prussia, even after age
and infirmities had increased upon him,
gave strict orders never to be allowed to
sleep later than four in the morning.
Peter the Great, whether at work in the
docks at London as a ship-carpenter, or
at the anvil as a blacksmith, or on the
throne of Russia, always arose before day-
light. Dr. Dwight used to tell his students that ' one hour of sleep before midnight is worth more than two hours after
that time.' If you ever hope to do anything in this world the habit of early rising *must* be formed, and the sooner it is
done the better."

6. *Keep yourself clean and neat in every
particular.* In this day there is no ex-

cuse for doing otherwise. But multitudes, especially among middle-aged men, practically ignore this goodly rule. It has been well said that " cleanliness is next to godliness." There is great virtue in soap and water vigorously applied. I do not believe in carrying bathing to an excess. Once or twice a week is often enough for a thorough bath with the majority of individuals. Of course there are exceptions to this rule. Day laborers and those who work at trades in which much dirt and sweat are the constant accompaniments should bathe every evening before retiring. A prolonged bath is not necessary—indeed it is injurious if oft-repeated. But a short bath, followed by a brisk rubbing with a coarse towel, is a splendid prelude to sweet, invigorating sleep. The water should be tepid—not too hot nor too cold. The temperature of the room should be likewise. Then there is no danger of taking cold.

Frequent ablutions of the hands and face during the day, aside from the more extensive baths recommended above, are always necessary. Every young man should keep his hands clean, his nails

carefully trimmed, his ears and neck spotless. And do not let dandruff accumulate
on your scalp and drop when combing
upon your coat. Keep your scalp white as
snow. If you have a diseased scalp, there
are various preparations obtainable which
will help you out. Keep your teeth clean.
Tooth brushes and healthful powders are
plentiful and cheap, and there are skilled
dentists almost everywhere. There is little excuse for the many foul breaths we so
often meet with nowadays caused from
defective or filty teeth. Strive to keep
your teeth and gums so clean and healthful that they will suggest "big white
drops of snow in banks of pretty pink
roses."

Watch your feet. If you have to wash
them twice a day and change your hose
every twenty-four hours, do so rather
than shock the olfactory nerves of everybody you meet. Some young men are
notorious for their stinking feet and foul
breath. Soap, water, and clean hose will
remedy the one, and total abstinence from
the filty weed and stomach-upsetting bowl
will go a long way toward remedying the
other.

Be neat and tidy in your dress, carefully avoiding all foppishness on the one hand and slovenliness on the other. No matter how poor you are financially, you can wear clean, neat clothes if you will. Never wear your undergarments too long without a change, and shun soiled linen as you would a plague. Keep your boots blackened. Let your necktie and handkerchief also be above reproach. Clothes do not make the man, but they often make the world's opinion of a man. The advice of President Fairchild to the students of the Kansas State Agricultural College, with reference to dress, is most wholesome: "Dress so as to excite no comment."

Some great men, 'tis true, have been notoriously uncouth and boorish in their personal habits. But these elements are not necessarily connected with superior ability. Johnson was great *in spite of* his contemptible manners, *not because of* them. "Keep your room and person at all times just as you would have it if you expected your mother or sister (or betrothed sweetheart) to make you a visit. Neatness is the word by which to designate all that is meant in regard to your personal appearance. Cleanliness is the first mark of politeness; it is agreeable to others, and is a very pleasant sensation to ourselves. The humor of Swift was not misapplied when he describes himself as recovering from sickness by changing his linen! A clean, neat appearance is always a good letter of introduction."

7. *Let constant development be your watchword.* Endeavor to develop both the outer and inner man to the highest possible pitch. Exercise is the key to victory in this matter. If you are a farmer, your body will get plenty of exercise following the plow, cutting the golden grain, or chopping the winter's wood. But unless you are of an exceptionally studious turn, you will be likely to neglect exercising the mind properly. If a student or clerk, the danger is reversed. But try to round up circumstances in such a manner as to make a rounded, consistently developed man of yourself. The farmer should spend an hour each day in reading and writing, and the professional man should spend as long a time in exercising. Let him take a run on his wheel, if he has

one, or row a boat. If he can have the
privileges of a gymnasium, good. If not,
a pleasant walk, or a brisk twenty-minutes'
run may be found exhilarating. George
Bancroft, the great historian, kept up his
daily horseback rides to a very advanced
age.

Take an interest in everything. Learn
something from everybody and everything. This was one of Henry Ward
Beecher's most prominent characteristics,
and played no small part in making him
one of America's greatest preachers. Garfield had a habit of never letting an opportunity pass to learn something. "Sir
Walter Scott gives us to understand,"
says Todd, "that he never met with any
man, let his calling be what it might,
from whom he could not, by a few moments' conversation, learn something
which he did not before know, and which
was valuable to him. This will account
for the fact that he seemed to have an
intuitive knowledge of everything. Who
but he would stop in the street and note
down a word which dropped among the
oaths of two angry men—a word for which
he had been looking for months? It is

quite as important to go through the world with the ears open as with the eyes open." "Old-fashioned economists," says another writer, "will tell you never to pass an old nail, or an old horse-shoe, or buckle, or even a pin, without taking it up; because, although you may not want it now, you will find a use for it some time or other. I say the same thing to you with regard to knowledge. However useless it may appear to you at the moment, seize upon all that is fairly within your reach. For there is not a fact within the whole circle of human observation, not even a fugitive anecdote that you read in a newspaper or hear in conversation that will not come into play some time or other; and occasions will arise when they involuntarily present their dim shadows in the train of your thinking and reasoning, as belonging to that train, and you will regret that you cannot recall them more distinctly."

A college education is a very desirable thing, and every young man should take a thorough course in some first-class institution if possible. But if from financial reasons or otherwise he cannot, let him not despair. Books are cheap, and every young man can possess a good library of his own by a little careful management. Great lecturers go almost everywhere nowadays, and the young man who really wants to learn has many excellent advantages within his reach on every hand.

8. *Give your most considerate attention to the soul.* "For what is a man profited if he shall gain the whole world and lose his own soul? or what shall a man give in exchange for his soul?" (Matt. 16: 26). There seems to be a growing disposition among young men to-day to slight religion, as though it were a matter somewhat beneath their dignified attention. It is estimated that only twenty-five per cent. of the young men of this country attend church. Three-fourths of our proud young voters lounge about the hotels. parks, drinking-places, etc., on Sunday, reading the dailies, talking politics, jesting, catching up odds and ends of business in store or office, speeding their horses, or doing some other equally soul-blighting thing. This is all wrong. It is high time the American people were

making the first day of the week a day of
rest and worship rather than a holiday.

Many young men read a little infidel
slush nowadays—not much, but just
enough to be able to talk smart when occasion presents itself. Mr. Ingersoll has
many admirers among this class. They
read nothing on the Christian side of
the question, and hence are unreasonable
in the extreme. Young man, don't make
a fool of yourself by belittling your mother's religion. Christianity is here to
stay, and the individual who arrays himself against it will find himself on the
losing side. Wm. E. Gladstone, England's greatest statesman, says: "The
greatest of all questions of the day is that
of the Gospel. It can and will correct
everything needing correction. All men
at the head of great movements are
Christian men. During the many years
I was Cabinet officer, I was brought into
association with sixty master minds, and
all but five of them were Christians."
Says Dr. Lowber in his "Cultura, "
"Daniel Webster said that the greatest
thought he ever had was his *personal responsibility to a personal God*. The great-

est thinkers of the world have taught that in every fully endowed man there is an instinctive obligation to a personal God." Don't be a half-baked human, young man. It may be amusing to a lot of hardened sinners who have very strong personal reasons for not believing in a hell to hear Mr. Ingersoll blaspheme God and the Bible for several hundred dollars a night. But it isn't manly, and it isn't safe. "Mr. Ingersoll is specially noted for his reckless statements about the Bible. He does not appear to respect any authority, and assumes positions that the scholarship of the world is clearly against. He ridicules Jehovah, but of course a son can make sport of his father when he wants to play the fool. Mr. Ingersoll says, 'Each nation has created a god, and the god has always resembled his creators.' That is certainly true of gods that men have made; but all scholars know that back of the polytheism of the nations there are traditions pointing to the true and living God. Man is so constituted that he will worship, and he becomes assimilated to the character of that which he worships. It is a fact that idolatrous

nations have never been able to extricate
themselves from idolatry. Truth had to
be presented from without, and that truth
was the Gospel of Christ as contained in
the Bible. You find no nation highly
civilized which does not believe in the
Bible. *The Bible and civilization go together.*"

While James Russell Lowell was our
minister to England, he once was present
at a public meeting in London when some
of the speakers of the evening expressed
their contempt for Christianity, saying
that they could "get along without it,
and depreciating its influence upon men."
Mr. Lowell volunteered a caustic reply to
their sophistries, a portion of which I
quote: "I do not think it safe," said the
distinguished poet, statesman, scholar.
"I am formulating no creed of my own;
I have always been a liberal thinker, and
have, therefore, allowed others who dif-
fered from me to think also as they liked;
but at the same time I fear that when we
indulge ourselves in the amusement of
going without a religion, we are not, perhaps, aware how much we are sustained
at present by an enormous mass, all about

us, of religious feeling and religious conviction; so that whatever it may be safe
for us to think—for us who have had
great advantages, and have been brought
up in such a way that a certain moral
direction has been given to our character,
—I do not know what would become of
the less-favored classes if they undertook
to play the same game. * * * The
worst kind of religion is no religion at all;
and these men, living in ease and luxury,
may be thankful that they live in lands
where the Gospel they neglect has tamed
the beastliness and ferocity of the men
who, but for Christianity, might long ago
have eaten their carcasses like the South
Sea Islanders, or cut off their heads and
tanned their hides like the monsters of
the French Revolution.

" When the microscopic search of skepticism, which has hunted the heavens and
sounded the seas to disprove the existence of a Creator, has turned its attention
to human society, and has found a place
on this planet, ten miles square, where a
decent man can live in decency, comfort
and security, supporting and educating his
children unspoiled and unpolluted; a place

where age is reverenced, infancy protected, manhood respected, womanhood honored, and human life held in due regard; when skepticism finds such a place ten miles square on this globe, where the Gospel of Christ has not gone and cleared the way, and laid the foundations, and made decency and security possible, it will then be in order for the skeptical *literati* to move thither, and there ventilate their views. But so long as these very men are dependent upon the religion that they discard for every privilege they enjoy, they may well hesitate a little before they seek to rob the Christian of his hope, and humanity of its faith in that Savior who alone has given to man that hope of eternal life which makes life tolerable and society possible, and robs death of its terrors and the grave of its gloom."

George Washington was a baptized believer in Christ. Abraham Lincoln was a devout believer in God. James A. Garfield was not only a believer, but a preacher of the Gospel. Judge Jeremiah Black, perhaps the greatest of American jurists, lived and died an earnest member of the Church of Christ. The young man who gives his heart to the Lamb of God will find himself in the best company the sun looks down upon. Saloon-keepers, anarchists, libertines, brawlers, and self-conceited sinners generally, make up the bulk of nineteenth-century infidelity. Keep your mind pure from doubts, my brother. Infidelity is a disgrace in Christian civilization—an unnatural and disgusting growth on modern progress. You can't afford to be a skeptic, for both temporal and eternal reasons. I beg of you, therefore, to lose no time in becoming a Christian, if you are not already one. Take the Bible, study it reverently, systematically, thoroughly. Do what it commands you to do in just the way it commands you to do it, and all will be well with you here and hereafter.

9. *Cultivate gentleness of disposition and sweetness of temper.* Don't be rough, careless, and unsociable. Don't allow yourself to get angry easily. Be self-reliant, but not too independent. Always be ready to " scatter seeds of kindness." Cheerfulness is one of the most commendable attributes a young man can possess. " Cheerfulness," says Bovee, " is an off-

shoot of goodness and wisdom." And Addison avers that "a cheerful temper joined with innocence will make beauty attractive, knowledge delightful, and wit good-natured." It is a glorious thing to always "look on the bright side." The world has a much keener appreciation for him who hopes than for him who despairs. So be gentle, sweet-tempered, hopeful under all circumstances. One fit of ill-temper may cost you a good position and a year's delay in your struggles toward success. A kind word never dies; neither does a saucy one. A word is a seed, and when sown is bound to bring forth a crop, good or bad, according to its nature. A bright face and a light heart is often a sure passport into the highest avenues of usefulness and felicity.

10. *Get married.* Not too soon; not too late in life. But at the proper time *get married*, for the word of God says, "It is not good that man should be alone." There is a disposition in certain circles nowadays to consider marriage a failure. But it seems to me very foolish for soured old maids or disappointed old bachelors to cry out against the sacred institution of marriage

which God ordained in the beginning, and
which he has blessed with choicest bene-
dictions in all ages. It is natural, scrip-
tural and right every way that man
should seek unto himself a wife. Usually
a man is but half a man until married.
Old-bachelorhood has been at a discount
in all nations and in all ages. "In past
ages," says Rev. John L. Brandt in his
"Marriage and the Home," "there have
been laws in various countries restricting
and punishing the bachelor. The laws of
Sparta allowed no man to marry until he
was thirty; then if he did not marry he
was compelled to march naked around the
market places singing songs composed
about him, and was not permitted to witness the gymnastic exercises of the maid-
ens. In Rome a heavier tax was levied
upon him, and he was not granted various
privileges extended to married men who
were fathers of several children. In England, occasionally, similar burdens have
been imposed upon him. The duty to
marry being imperative and the penalty
for not marrying so heavy make it certain that bachelors were very scarce during the earlier centuries." But they are

more plentiful now than ever before, owing to the selfishness of man, and false
notions concerning fitness for marriage.
There are, perhaps, some valid reasons
for not marrying. Mr. Brandt suggests
four:

1st. "Those noble sons and brothers
who are providing for widowed mothers
and dependent sisters have valid reasons
for not marrying. In years to come, when
mother's gray hairs are laid away in the
tomb, and when the sisters are provided
for, God may lead them to one who has
been waiting for them. It will pay any
girl to wait years for such a man; he is a
blessing to society, and when the time
comes he will make a kind and provident
husband.

2d. "Some men should not marry because of physical debility. Some are de-
formed; some inherit objectionable physical ailments and weak constitutions, who
had better remain single.

3d. "Some should not marry because
of the bodily disease and corruption they
have brought on themselves through their
vicious habits. Think of a man who has
lived in debauchery and licentiousness

for ten years, offering himself to a spotless woman as a husband! The very proposition is an insult. Such a depraved beast has no right to marry. You might as well join a skunk to a lamb, as to join a diseased man of this type to a virtuous woman.

4th. " Some men should not marry because they are unable to dwell with their wives. Soldiers, sailors, and missionaries who are required by their vocations to be absent from home ninety-nine days in every hundred ought not to marry. Husbands who are always absent from home keep wives in anxiety and suspense. I would add that men who spend the majority of their evenings at clubs and saloons when they should be at home had better have remained single, because they give much uneasiness and unhappiness to their wives."

But no young man should keep out of matrimony simply because he fears he cannot support a wife as royally as he would like, or because his salary forbids their shining with brilliance in social life, or because he is too lazy and mean and selfish to shoulder the cares of a home and

family. There is no nobler ambition for a
young man to have than that of creating
a happy home from which shall ever flow
truth, purity and love to bless this cold,
careless, sin-ridden world.

Concerning the age at which a young
man should marry, authorities are very far
apart in their opinions. Lord Beaconsfield says: "For myself I believe that permanent union of the sexes should be en-
couraged; nor do I conceive that general
happiness can ever flourish but in societies
where it is the custom for males to marry
at eighteen." Dr. Cowan, in his "Science
of a New Life," favors an age of from
twenty-eight to thirty. I am inclined to
think that a happy mean would be much
better. Most young men would be infinitely better off if they would marry between twenty-one and twenty-five. A
happy marriage at this age will save many
a man from bad habits. Richter declares
that "no man can live piously or die
righteously without a wife." A boarding-
house life is not usually conducive to
moral growth. Set up a home, young
man! Set up a home!!

Concerning the selection of a wife, and

other important matters allow me to quote the following suggestions from the racy and sensible pen of Dr. Dio Lewis:—

" Do not select a woman with a temperament very similar to your own. You may judge of temperament by the color of the hair and skin, and by the shape of the body and intensity of the nervous system. *Do not select a woman with a forehead shaped like your own.* If you are large, do not marry a small woman. The disparity in size should not be great. The several reasons for this advice are too obvious to need mention. Such an error among animals often proves fatal, and indeed it often does among human beings. Avoid a small waist as you would the plague. Do not marry an invalid. What you want is not a patient to nurse, but a *helpmeet.* If you join your fortunes to those of a pale, nervous, cold-blooded, fainting creature, you will spend the rest of your life in bemoaning your folly. Do not choose your mate from a family cursed with epilepsy, insanity, or consumption.

" Do not select an over-dressed woman. Excess of jewelry and other ornaments shows a weakness, not to say vice, intoler-

able in your nearest friend and companion.
It is vulgar and cheap, and is never found
in superior persons. Shun the untidy as
you would an open drain. Give an un-
loving daughter a wide berth. Avoid ignorant girls, and those with excessive accomplishments. If in this country a young
woman is exceptionally ignorant it proves
a lack of capacity, while an excess of accomplishments shows a certain light-
headedness, a certain lack of the plain,
substantial qualities which are so desirable in a life-long companion. Avoid very
homely and very handsome women. If
your choice is very ugly, she will constantly wound your taste in yourself and
in your children; and if she is very beautiful, all the men in the neighborhood will
be likely to find it out, and some of them
may tell her about it, or she may chance
to look in the glass and discover it herself. Do not marry your cousin. Your
wife should be over twenty years of age.

"Be perfectly frank in comparing your
tastes and principles, your aspirations,
hopes and aims, *before marriage.* You
should take especial pains to do so, that
you may not commit the sad mistake of

tying together uncongenial natures —of
yoking 'incompatibles.' There must be
mutual concessions all along, to insure
harmony and final unity of even the most
congenial; but oil and water had better not
attempt to blend,—it is against nature,
and the trial will result in failure. When
the ceremony is over, and you have retired
to your chamber, make a little speech to
your wife. The following will do: 'My
Precious Companion: During our courtship, we have been very happy. It has
been the supreme joy of my life. We both
feel that in possessing each other we have
secured our greatest good. The instinct
which underlies this love between husband and wife would quickly disappear if
we gave ourselves up to the unrestrained
indulgences of passion. As we prize this
precious love, we must not only avoid excess, but we must preserve our delicacy
and modesty.'

"And now let me whisper an important
secret in your ear. You have an income
of a hundred dollars a month, more or
less. Your wife has no separate income.
Put your money in the upper little drawer
in your bureau. Have a carpenter put on

a fine lever lock with two keys. Give
your wife one and keep the other yourself.
Say to her, ' *Our* money is in that drawer;
help yourself.' Not three wives in a hundred will spend too much. Three out of
four will spend too little, and you will
have to urge them to use more, and that
will increase your mutual love. That
little drawer will prevent half the troubles
between husband and wife. It is sure to
prevent all extravagance. Those little
keys will unlock your mutual confidence."

O, blessed be matrimony! Blessed be
home! Young man, don't say you can't
afford to marry. That excuse is born of
satan. If you are a pure, true man, and
desire to remain so, you can't afford not
to marry. Longfellow spoke wisely when
he said,

> " As unto the bow the cord is,
> So unto the man is woman:
> Though she bends him, she obeys him;
> Though she draws him, yet she follows;
> Useless each without the other!"

But enough, my brother. Go back now
and read these ten suggestions again.
Meditate upon them. Then arise and put
them into practice, and you will not fail
of attaining unto happiness—the chief
desire of man—both here and hereafter.

CHAPTER X.

PRIVATE WORDS TO MARRIED MEN.

"A good wife is heaven's best gift to man; his angel of mercy—minister of graces innumerable; his gem of many virtues. Her economy his safest steward, her lips his faithful counselors, and her prayers the ablest advocates of heaven's blessings on his head."—*Jeremy Taylor.*

"Husbands, love your wives." In this day of dissipation and divorce, no better advice can be given than that. Love covers a multitude of faults. A wife's love seldom wanes and dies, but a husband's often does. Things ought not so to be. A husband's love, like the wife's, should wax stronger and sweeter with each passing year. If a wife's love fails, it is usually the husband's fault. If every married man would do his duty, there would not be one divorce to-day where there are ten.

Some men attribute the cause of all their meanness to an incompatible wife. There may be a few instances in the world where this is the case. But, as a rule, an unhappy husband has no one to blame but himself. Nine women out of ten possess remarkable adaptability. They follow lovingly, uncomplainingly and happily wherever the husband leads. Bad man is he, therefore, who does not keep his face toward the light, and his feet in the straight and narrow path which leads onward and upward toward a better development every way. "A good young wife," says Rev. Brandt, "may be made by a cruel, extravagant, neglectful, improvident husband, a bad wife and mother. The education of the wife is three times out of four the work of the husband. If wives have to submit to their husbands, the husbands should be governed by reason and religion. They should honor and respect their wives if they would receive in return love and obedience."

To be happily married, and to remain so through life, is man's highest lot in this world. Permit a few suggestions, therefore, which I believe will help toward this end:

1. *Have a home.* Don't board. Your wife, like all true women, is largely en-

dowed with the home-instinct. She sighs for a little bower of her own, which she can fix up cozily for the choice of her heart. Give her a chance. No young married couple should board. If not able at first to buy and furnish a house, rent. Even though you have to put up with a few rooms scantily furnished, it is infinitely better that you should be AT HOME than to live around boarding-houses. Wife will be much more contented, and so will you. Pen can not do justice to the joy you will experience when you come home from work at six in the evening and find your beloved waiting at the gate to welcome you. How your steps will quicken and your heart flutter as you catch the first glance of her! With a loving kiss and trustful pressure of the hand, she will lead you into your little sitting-room, and while chatting incessantly, assist in removing hat and coat, preparatory to an invitation to the evening meal. Notice how neat and well arranged everything is about the rooms. Speak of it. It will send a thrill of pleasure through your darling's heart, which will manifest itself upon her pretty cheeks. Notice how be-

comingly but unfeignedly she is attired.
Speak of that too. A woman loves a
little praise, and usually deserves much
more than she receives of this invaluable
article. When you go into your little
dining-room, and see the table spread for
two—everything just right—be careful or
you'll upset something from excessive
nervousness! Oh, what white bread!
What good steak! What pie! Speak of
it. Tell your young wife that your
mother was a fine cook, but she never
beat that. It will add several links to the
chain of affection that already binds her
heart to yours. The very thought of
putting up at a boarding-house spoils this
picture you see. Don't do it. Start out
determined to have a home, and let nothing great or small thwart this purpose.

Don't live with your relatives, no matter
how rich they are and how good an offer
they make you—don't live with your kin
on either side. It has been well said that
no house is large enough for two families.
Live alone and you'll always think more
of your relatives, and they of you.

Lose no time in owning your home. It
is a bad thing to be always renting. It

breeds restlessness and shiftlessness. In
this day of so many excellent building and
loan associations, almost any pair can
have a home of their own. When you own
the place where you live, you will both
take pride in improving it and making it
pleasant and attractive. This will add to
your mutual happiness. A home of flowers,
music, sunshine and domestic tranquillity
—what a foretaste of that home above, a
home not made with hands, eternal in the
heavens!

2. *Keep yourself busy.* This is necessary for many reasons. If you are poor
financially, it is necessary for you to work
hard and incessantly in order to support
your family. If, however, you are rich,
it is necessary for you to work just the
same to hold what you have, and also to
keep yourself from the dangers of idleness.
The true man is "happiest when busiest,
and busiest when happiest." To be able
to work is one of the choicest of man's
prerogatives. "No young lady should
think of accepting the hand of a young
man who has no trade, business or profession by which he can maintain a family.
A do-nothing young man will make a good-

for-nothing husband. It is a grave mistake to launch the boat without being able to pilot it. It is much safer to have a poor and industrious man than a rich and indolent one. An idle man struggles through life to little purpose. No man can afford to be idle. A habit of industry once formed is not apt to be lost. The industrious man will command respect; he will descend to no meanness; he will be provident for the future; he will keep want from the door, wood on the pile, flour in the barrel, provisions in the pantry, and cheer in the heart."

3. *Be trustful, gallant, faithful.* Make your wife your best and truest earth-friend indeed. Keep nothing from her. Secrecy has no place between the loyal husband and his wife.

Treat your wife as gallantly as you always treated her when she was your sweetheart. It is amazing how much this will do toward increasing your mutual affection. Keep up your courtship. I know a man and his wife who, although married years ago, and although they have children growing up about them, are courting yet. They take as much pleasure in going out together, in making each other little presents and surprises, and in practioing the many little gallantries usually observed only by lovers, as they did when single. And it is the happiest pair I ever saw.

Be as true to your wife in every respect as the needle to the pole. Unfaithfulness on your part is just as much a sin, whether you consider it so or not, as unfaithfulness on her part. Don't be too prolific with your attentions to other ladies. Be courteous, sociable, friendly, nothing more. Too many married men are excessively gallant toward other ladies.

Don't be jealous, nor suspicious. Your wife isn't going to run off with some other fellow. If she should be inclined that way, the sooner she goes the better for you. Jealousy is well named the "green-eyed monster." Suspicion is its twin curse. Don't let them inside your doors.

4. *Be temperate in sexual intercourse.* This is a subject upon which there have been many foolish things written. I trust I am not an extremist either way on this question. I believe that sexual inter-

course is a natural and healthful act, and
therefore no more sinful for husband and
wife to engage in than eating, drinking,
sleeping or in any other reasonable exercise. But as every right-thinking man
realizes the essentiality of temperance in
eating, drinking and sleeping, so every
sensible husband realizes the imperative
importance of temperance in sexual intercourse. I do not for a moment accept
the theory advanced by some writers that
the sexual act should not be engaged in
except when offspring is desired. But I
believe with Dr. Guernsey that "these
sexual unions serve to bring the married
pair into a perfectly harmonious relation
to each other," and hence are intended by
our Maker for other high and holy purposes along with that of begetting children. "The sexual relation is one of the
most important uses of married life; it
vivifies the affections for each other as
nothing else in this world can, and is a
powerful reminder of the mutual obligations of husband and wife to each other,
and the community in which they live.
Indulgence, however, should not be too
frequent, lest it debilitate the pair, and

undermine their health. The bridegroom and husband should watch over his bride and wife to see that she is not a sufferer, and should govern himself accordingly."

Over-indulgence brings on a multitude of evils. "Some of the most common effects of sexual excess," says Dr. Dio Lewis, "are backache, lassitude, giddiness, dimness of sight, noises in the ears, numbness of the fingers, and paralysis. The drain is universal, but the more sensitive organs and tissues suffer most. So the nervous system gives way, and continues the principal sufferer throughout. A very large part of the premature loss of sight and hearing, dizziness, numbness and pricking in the hands and feet, and other kindred developments, are all justly chargeable to unbridled venery. Not infrequently I see in a single hour more than one man whose head or back or nerves testify to such reckless expenditure."

A great many men seem to think that a marriage certificate means license to go to any length desired in the indulgence of passion. But this is a grave mistake. The marriage certificate does not give a man the moral right, whatever may be

said on the legal side of the question, to
make a slave of his wife and a fool of himself. I verily believe that a large percentage of the cases of vertigo, backache,
kidney, stomach and liver disorders, nervousness and consumption are brought
on by excessive sexual intercourse. In
such instances a change of climate or
patent medicines will not effect a cure.
Total abstinence for a few months, and
afterwards a very limited indulgence, is
the only sensible course.

" 'How often may I indulge myself ?' is
a question the physician who gives attention to sexual troubles hears every day,"
says Dr. Lewis. " It is a point most difficult to settle by any general rule. Here
is A., twenty-five years old, just married,
a farmer, with an iron constitution and no
nerves. *He* asks the question. Now
comes B., fifty years old, with delicate
constitution, the editor of a morning paper, dyspeptic, and all nerves. And *he*
asks the *same* question. A tri-daily indulgence would prove less disastrous to
A. than a tri-monthly indulgence to B.
How is it possible to generalize?"

Jeremy Taylor, in a chapter entitled,

"Rules for Married Persons, or Matrimonial Chastity," wisely remarks that, "In their permissions and license the husband and wife must be sure to observe the order of nature and the ends of God. *He is an ill husband that uses his wife as a man treats a harlot, having no other end but pleasure.* Concerning which our best rule is that although in this, as in eating and drinking, there is an appetite to be satisfied, which cannot be done without pleasing that desire; yet, since that desire and satisfaction were intended by nature for other ends, they should never be separated from those ends, but always be joined with all or one of these ends: *with a desire for children; or to avoid fornication; or to lighten and ease the cares and sadness of household affairs;* or to *endear each other;* but never with a purpose, either in act or desire, to separate the sensuality from these ends which hallow it."

Every husband and wife, after thoughtful and reverent consideration, must themselves settle this question of frequency. I would emphasize the words *and wife*, for I hold it to be man's duty to govern his

actions in this matter not by his own desires, but by his companion's. Her right
to say when and under what circumstances she shall engage in this important act,
which may result in maternity, should be
held sacred. There is little, if any, danger of a loving wife being too strict with
her heart's idol in this matter. And there
is also little danger of a thoughtful wife's
being too lenient with her husband if the
matter is left lovingly and uncomplainingly
to her judgment. Let this rule be universally adopted, and I believe domestic
felicity would be revolutionized for good.
There would be fewer stoop-shouldered,
flat-chested, coughing wives in the world
—wives from whom the bloom of health
has gone forever because of the unbridled
passions of thoughtless and relentless
husbands. O, watch fondly over the
health and happiness of your wife, my
brother! It will pay you a thousandfold.
Re-read this paragraph and then govern
yourself accordingly. You may not have
nearly so many indulgences in the future
as in the past if you do, but what you do
have will be all the sweeter, holier, and
healthier. O, "be temperate in all things!"

5. *Sleep alone.* This may appear at first cruel advice, but it is physiological. Prominent writers have given this matter serious attention, and earnestly recommended that husbands and wives should sleep apart. "Married people make a great mistake in allowing themselves to sleep together," says a prominent New York physician. "This practice leads in a measure to uncongeniality. From five to eight hours' bodily contact in every twenty-four with one person not only causes an equalization of those magnetic elements which, when diverse in quantity and quality, produce physical attraction and passional love, but it promotes permanent uncongeniality by making the married pair grow alike physically. The interchange of individual electricities, and the absorption of each other's exhalations, lead directly to temperamental inadaptation, and to this cause may be ascribed one of the chief reasons why a husband and wife manifest such a tendency to grow alike after many years of matrimonial companionship. The *Laws of Life*, commenting on this subject, remarks that 'more quarrels arise between brothers, be-

tween sisters, between hired girls, between school-girls, between clerks in
stores, between apprentices in mechanic
shops, between hired men, between husbands and wives, owing to electrical
changes through which their nervous
systems go by lodging together night after
night under the same bedclothes, than
by any other disturbing cause. There is
nothing that will so derange the nervous
system of a person who is eliminative in
nervous force as to lie all night in bed
with another person who is absorbent in
nervous force. The absorbee will go to
sleep and rest all night, while the elimin-
ator will be tumbling and tossing, restless
and nervous, and wake up in the morning
fretful, peevish, fault-finding and discouraged. No two persons, no matter who
they are, should habitually sleep together.
One will thrive and the other will lose.
This is the law; but in married life it is
defied almost universally.'

"In corroboration of what is stated in
the quotation," continues this authority,
"I may say that I have been informed
hundreds of times by husbands who have
consulted me that they felt ever so much

better when absent from home, or when by some incidental causes they slept apart from their wives; and quite as many married women have reported precisely the same results regarding their experience when rooming with or without their husbands. It is evidently far from being a whim, or it would not be entertained by so many people who have no social intercourse or acquaintance by which to originate it and report it uniformly. The statement comes from quarters too diverse to allow the charge to be made that it is a morbid fancy or a local contagion, which originally sprang from the imagination of some nervous old lady. A reform in this custom, however, can hardly be expected to be made in one generation. Husbands and wives who have been in the practice of sleeping together for from five to thirty years will hardly be persuaded to relinquish the social luxury of spending their nights together, especially if their matrimonial life has led to a fair amount of social enjoyment. The retiring chit-chat, and the morning helps of a little pinning or brushing, and aid in buttoning or hooking, are little affairs, but great in the aggregate, and not to be easily set aside. And 'even the habit of feeling a companion by one's side during the waking moments, or when turning over, is one which cannot be given up by some without passing many restless or sleepless nights in getting used to it. For all persons, however, who are disposed to undertake a partial reform in this matter, the plain people of Germany have a practice which might be adopted as a sort of compromise. A newspaper writer speaks of it as follows: 'The married people of plain life sleep in two single beds, each being a sweet little isle of its own, while the two are affectionately contiguous. The connubial neighbors can respectfully shake hands, and wish good-night and good-morning. But the territory of each is distinct; the clothes of each are cut separate; each bed is complete, and there is no continuousness of bolster, or implied community of pillow.' The adoption of this custom would be a step in the right direction."

6. *Have children.* There is a growing disposition at large to-day not to have children if it can possibly be avoided.

Not infrequently a young married couple envy an older married pair who have lived together for fifteen years or so without children. "What do they do?" is the question. In other words, how do they prevent nature having her way? So common is the practice of abortion to-day that one authority declares that we are "rapidly becoming a nation of murderers."

In olden times it was considered the greatest calamity that could befall a woman to remain childless through life. It ought to be so to-day; for child-bearing is noble, healthful, and right every way. Children fill the home with sunshine. They give us something to live for. They mellow our hearts with love, joy, and sympathy.

> "Ah! what would the world be to us
> If the children were no more?
> We should dread the desert behind us
> Worse than the darkness before."
> —*Longfellow.*

When a man is tired from the duties of the day, or heavy-hearted from disappointment, his best tonic is the touch of his baby's little chubby hand and the prattle of his darling ones at play, while gentle, loving mamma is near. "I must counsel husbands and wives to cherish the hope of becoming parents," says Rev. Brandt in a lecture on "Model Parents," "and to let their hearts stand in a holy attitude in this respect. You should allow neither moderate income, financial pressure, sensual pleasures, nor evil forebodings, to cause you to entertain unholy thoughts or induce you to engage in criminal proceedings in this matter. No child should be considered an unwelcome intruder in the home. The heart of the home is the cradle; it is the cementing tie between husband and wife. God intends that husbands and wives should become parents; *and no pure woman or honorable man will enter upon matrimony with intentions to the contrary.* If they do, God will visit upon them degraded morals, ruined health, financial loss, or other terrible afflictions. The world has millions of faithful wives and mothers, but there are thousands of childless wives who are so because they entered into that black crime of conspiring with the devil to prevent them from being mothers. They regard children as an unmitigated nuisance and consequently darken, blast, and damn their own lives with an act of murder. On the other hand, God blesses the mothers, in that He prolongs their days and brings up their children to reflect honor and glory upon them."

"The object of marriage," says Dr. Guernsey, "is the ultimation of that love which brings the two together, and binds them together in the procreation and rearing of children for heaven. This is the only true aim and sole object about which every earthly desire, interest, and plan of the married pair should cluster. No greater crime in the sight of heaven exists to-day than that of perverting the natural uses of marriage. This is done in a great variety of ways, every one of which is criminal, in whatever form practiced; and none will escape the penalty—no, not one. Nature's laws are inexorable; every transgression thereof is surely punished, even at the *climacteric period*, if not before. The question of too frequent conceptions is a matter for the investigation, advice, and decision of an experienced, judicious and upright physician. It should never be taken in hand and judged upon by the parties themselves. And to the objection: 'I can't afford to have children; they cost too much,' I have faith enough to reply: Our Heavenly Father never sends more mouths than He can feed. Let each one do his and her duty in life and this cavil falls to the ground. Good people everywhere rejoice when they behold a married couple living together in an orderly manner, and rearing a large family of children. How often is Queen Victoria held up as a pattern of excellence in this respect; she accepted and acknowledged Prince Albert as her husband and gave herself to him as his wife; and so indeed she was, in every sense of the term. Although a queen, sitting on the pinnacle of power, she did not seek to avoid the pangs, the dangers, or inconveniences of child-bearing. By her own personal strength her twelve children were brought forth, and her own sensitive fibres and tissues felt the suffering. She nursed, caressed, and loved them like a good mother, and she was a *royal mother!* Other kings and queens have done likewise; other husbands and wives, high in power, wealth and fashion, have done and are still doing the same. And how much the less should we, in the humbler walks of life, obey the Divine command, ' Be fruitful and multiply.' If a husband truly loves his wife, and if she truly loves him, they will live for each other, and in each other—they will be *one;* and they will seek to do right in every particular in their marital relation.''

> " There is a sight all hearts beguiling—
> A youthful mother to her infant smiling
> Who, with spread arms, and dancing feet,
> And cooing voice, returns its answer sweet.''
> —*Bailley.*

In this connection, I want to speak of one method of preventing conception which I fear is very commonly used. I refer to the practice commonly called by medical writers " Onanism.'' It consists of withdrawing the male member in copulation just before the act is complete, and spilling the seed on the outside of the female organ. There is only one case of this kind recorded in the Bible, and in that instance the Lord killed the guilty man, Onan (see Gen. 38: 1-10). It goes without saying that this is a nasty, vulgar practice, and no decent man should ever think of engaging in anything so shameful. Physicians are agreed that this practice long continued will result in the same direful calamities following self-abuse, for it really is one form of that loathsome sin.

6. *Be a Christian.* There are multitudes of homes where the husband and father is not a Christian. The wife and mother is: but oh! how hard and lonely is the upward way to her when the dearest of all earth-friends will not travel that way with her! It is not enough, my brother, to pay her preacher a little now and then, or spend a little change at the church festival. There is too much of this "leaning against the church" on the part of husbands whose wives are Christians. Why don't you go in and be done with it? Don't stand around outside. Your wife can't go to Heaven for you. Christian service is an individual matter. It can be rendered alone, 'tis true; but it is so much easier when loved ones walk with us in the heavenward path.

Dear reader, if you are not a Christian, I beg of you give this matter your immediate attention. Life is uncertain and very short at best; death is on our track, and eternity is long. The Bible tells us that we are all to be judged "according to the deeds done in the body." Are you ready for judgment? There is only one way to heaven. Christ says, "I am the way." The Apostle Peter assures us that "there is no other name under heaven given among men whereby we may be saved; neither is there salvation in any other" than Christ. (Acts 4: 12.) If you are not a Christian, you are in a lost state. No matter who you are, nor where you hail from, you have no hope out of Christ. Distinguished birth can not avail in your salvation; nor wealth, nor honor, nor learning. All these things are good if consecrated to the Lord, but otherwise they are worse than filthy rags, for of themselves they can do naught but intensify eternal punishment. Why depend upon human gifts for redemption! *Christ alone can save.*

Why not become a Christian to-day? To-morrow may be too late. God has nowhere promised us another day in which to repent. He says, "*Now is the accepted time: To-day is the day of salvation!*"

Every time we breathe, two persons die somewhere. Your time may come soon. Are you ready? At the great Lisbon earthquake it is estimated that sixty thousand persons perished in six minutes. Few of the number were ready to die. We ought to live every hour as though it would be our last upon earth.

The terms of salvation are very simple. No miracle is necessary in conversion. It is a shame that many theologians have thrown a cloud of mysticism about the Christian religion. But be assured, dear unsaved reader, that the way to God is clear and easy. 1st, *Hear the Word* (Matt. 17: 5). 2d, *Believe* (John 3: 16). 3d, *Repent* (Acts 17: 30). 4th, *Confess Christ* (Matt. 10: 32). 5th, *Be baptized* (Acts 2: 38). Take these five steps prayerfully and sincerely, and your sins will be forgiven, you will be a member of the Church of Christ, a Christian, and an heir to eternal glory. Then "add to faith virtue; and to virtue knowledge; and to knowlege temperance; and to temperance patience; and to patience godliness; and to godliness brotherly kindness; and to brotherly kindness charity (II Pet. 1: 5-7).

In short, take the Bible as your guide. Do what it tells you to do in the way it tells you to do it. Just *believe and obey*. That's all there is to do in following Christ.

What is better in this world than a Christian home, where father and mother both read the Word of God regularly and pray? Where a meal is never eaten without thanksgiving? Where the children are taught to say,

> " Now I lay me down to sleep:
> I pray the Lord my soul to keep.
> If I should die before I wake,
> I pray the Lord my soul to take.
> This I ask for Jesus' sake?"

Where husband and wife on bended knees together commune with God, and arise strengthened for all the duties of life? Where good papers and books, inspiring music and refining conversation give each inmate of this little "paradise on earth " a precious foretaste of that glorious state beyond?

My brother, you can have such a home if you will. You can't afford to do without Christ. He came into the world to dry away tears, bind up broken hearts,

and clothe the face with sunshine. He
wants us to be happy. Nobody but a Christian ought to be happy. So come to
Him! Trust Him! Serve Him! Be a
true, pure man! Be a Christian! Live
not for self alone; but live for God and for
humanity. So shall your life be useful
and fruitful. You have lost much by your
mistakes and sins in the past perhaps;
but "let the dead past bury its dead."
Turn to the future, and go on lovingly,
trustfully, determinedly, happily, and the
Lord will crown you with loving kind-
nesses innumerable. With James Whit-
comb Riley I would say,

> "Oh, heart of mine, we shouldn't
>   Worry so!
> What we've missed of calm we couldn't
>   Have, you know!
> What we've met of stormy rain
> And of sorrow's driving pain,
> We can better meet again
>   If it blow.

> "We have erred in that dark hour
>   We have known,
> When the tears fell with the shower
>   All alone—
> Were not shine and shower blent
> As the gracious Master meant?
> Let us temper our content
>   With His own.

"For we know not every morrow
        Can be sad;
So, forgetting all the sorrow
        We have had,
Let us fold away our fears,
And put by our foolish tears,
And through all the coming years
        Just be glad."

What Distinguished Critics Say.

From JUDGE CHAS. J. SCOFIELD, The Noted Juror and Novelist.

"Plain Points on Personal Purity," by Geo. F. Hall, the well-known preacher, author and evangelist, wins its way to the attention of the reader by the significance of the title, and the attractiveness of the exterior, and holds that attention by the importance of the themes discussed, the fearlessness with which sin is exposed and denounced, and the clear, forcible language, which is a fitting vehicle for every thought, suggestion, warning and exhortation. Mr. Hall is a bold, independent thinker. He falters not in the proclamation of the whole truth. When he undertakes to oppose the vices of men, he hesitates not to lift the veil and make a full exposure. The book will mainly be a glad message of hope and warning to many. Let every Christian worker circulate it extensively, and thus assist in showing men what they are and how they may become better. —*Chas. J. Scofield.*

From PROF. DAVID SWING, The Eminent Chicago Divine

Your book on "Personal Purity" seems written with so much good taste, and with such logical force, that it ought to be accepted as a valuable book for the age. Not less valuable than the last half of the volume is the argument against tobacco—that humbug of the world. —*David Swing.*

From J. V. UPDIKE, The Great Evangelist.

Your book is great. I was surprised by it. It should be read and heeded by every man and boy in this or any other country. It should be translated into the different languages, advertised in all the papers and magazines in the country, and sold on all trains by everybody who would do the human family good. If you should die now, you have your monument in this book. It is plain, pointed, personal and exceedingly practical and thorough. Most men who read it will say, "That hits me hard." May God bless it in its mission for good. —*J. V. Updike.*

From F. M. RAINS, Managing Editor of the Christian Standard.

I have read "Plain Points on Personal Purity" with interest and profit. It is a bold stroke at a great evil, and the book ought to have a very wide sale. I have no doubt that, carefully read, it will accomplish great good. You richly deserve the thanks of all who are interested in a nobler manhood. At $1.25 per copy the book is a marvel of cheapness. —*F. M. Rains.*

From PROF. E. M. HUTTO, Superintendent of Schools, Stillwater, Oklahoma.

It should be in the hands of every teacher in the land. My experience in the school-room has brought me face to face with many of the startling truths so forcibly pictured in this book. Considering the great opportunity teachers in our public schools have for disseminating knowledge on most of the subjects treated upon in this work, there is certainly a grave responsibility resting upon us. "Plain Points" will force one to a sense of his duty, and help him in the performance of it. —*E. M. Hutto.*

From DR. M. L. DOOM, The Scholarly and Successful Specialist.

Have examined "Plain Points on Personal Purity" with great care, and pronounce it the best work on the subject extant, displaying a wonderful knowledge of physiological life—truthful, chaste and attractive. Such a work cannot fail to receive the endorsement of the entire medical profession. —*M. L. Doom, M. D.*

From J. W. ALLEN, Pastor West Side Church of Christ, Chicago.

The best description of Niagara Falls was written by one who never saw them. The author of this book was never in a saloon, never smoked a cigar, nor played a card, and from his youth up has kept the seventh commandment; yet it would be difficult to find these evils more truthfully or startlingly portrayed than he has here portrayed them. The best teachers of morals are not reformed drunkards and converted prize fighters. He who teaches purity should himself be pure; and this, no doubt, is the reason why this book is a clean handling of things unclean, and startles while it does not stain. Every young man in this land should read it; every preacher should load up with it and fire away, point blank, at the book does at the startling sins of the sterner sex." There ought to be more, and plainer, and braver preaching along these lines. Mechanically, as in other respects, the book is a gem, and we can conscientiously and earnestly commend it to all as a clean, clean, courageous book. —*J. W. Allen.*